Voice

IN THE AMERICAN WEST

Andy Wilkinson
Series Editor

ALSO IN THE SERIES

Cowboy's Lament: A Life on the Open Range
Frank Maynard; edited by Jim Hoy

The Hell-Bound Train: A Cowboy Songbook, Second Edition
Glenn Ohrlin; edited by Charlie Seemann

If I Was a Highway
Michael Ventura

In My Father's House: A Memoir of Polygamy
Dorothy Allred Solomon

Llano Estacado: An Island in the Sky
Stephen Bogener and William Tydeman, editors

Light in the Trees
Gail Folkins

Rightful Place
Amy Hale Auker

A Sweet Separate Intimacy: Women Writers of the American Frontier, 1800–1922
Susan Cummins Miller, editor

Texas Dance Halls: A Two-Step Circuit
Gail Folkins and J. Marcus Weekley

ON BECOMING APACHE

On Becoming Apache

Conger Beasley Jr.
Harry Mithlo

TEXAS TECH UNIVERSITY PRESS

This book is typeset in Walbaum MT Std.
The paper used in this book meets the minimum requirements of ANSI/NISO Z39.48-1992 (R1997).
∞

Designed by Hannah Gaskamp

Cover photograph by Nicholas Swanson

Frontis illustration: Charles Banks Wilson, *Search for the Native American Purebloods*, 3rd Edition, University of Oklahoma Press. First published 1983 by Stoval Museum of Science and History.

Library of Congress Cataloging-in-Publication Data
Names: Mithlo, Harry, author. | Beasley, Conger, Jr., author.
Title: On becoming Apache / Harry Mithlo, Conger Beasley Jr.
Other titles: Voice in the American West.
Description: Lubbock: Texas Tech University Press, 2020. | Series: Voice in the American West | Summary: "The story of Watson Mithlo, Chiricahua Apache, narrated in three voices; chronicles how the Chiricahua were relocated from Arizona to Florida to Alabama and finally to Fort Sill, Oklahoma"—Provided by publisher.
Identifiers: LCCN 2020003824 | ISBN 9781682830598 (paperback)
Subjects: LCSH: Mithlo, Watson. | Chiricahua Indians—Oklahoma—Biography. | Prisoners of war—Biography. | LCGFT: Biographies.
Classification: LCC E99.C68 M58 2020 | DDC 976.6/004972560092 [B]—dc23
LC record available at https://lccn.loc.gov/2020003824

ISBN: 978-1-68283-059-8 (paper)
Printed in the United States of America
20 21 22 23 24 25 26 27 28 / 9 8 7 6 5 4 3 2 1
Texas Tech University Press
Box 41037
Lubbock, Texas 79409-1037 USA
800.832.4042
ttup@ttu.edu
www.ttupress.org

For Michael Mithlo Jr.
(October 11, 1988–August 8, 2016)

Watson Mithlo, Chiricahua Apache; portrait by Charles Banks Wilson, 1981.

ON BECOMING APACHE

HARRY

The sand-colored brick Indian United Methodist Church, located on the south bank of Cache Creek outside the rural town of Apache, Oklahoma, can barely contain the crowd of people who have come to pay their respects to Watson "Bill" Mithlo, Chiricahua Apache Prisoner of War, as he lies in a steel-blue casket.

The sanctuary filled early with mourners on a sweltering July afternoon in 1993, and now the crowd has spilled onto the grounds outside the church. The people have come to see the family; the people have come to see the mourners; the people have come to see the remains of this venerable 107-year-old Apache warrior, medicine man, cowboy, rancher, historian, story-teller, husband and father — my Dad — put to rest in Mother Earth.

The people packed inside the church are dressed in a variety of clothes, from colorful native dress to casual blue jeans to formal business suits. They have come from all over the country, from all directions where the four winds blow. They crowd into the church until it seems as if the church can't hold any more, and still they come.

As the service begins, they press closer to the open back walls and side doors of the church, straining to hear what the Reverend Sam Batise, a Choctaw Indian Methodist minister, is saying as he opens the service in our native Apache language. The people inside join him in singing the ancient hymns, which rise and fall on the mournful drift of their unaccompanied voices.

Inside the church, sitting with my family in a front-row seat, I watch my brother, Melvin Mithlo, a young medicine man, bless our father with sacred pollen husked from cattail stalks. His long, black braids sway with his body as he bends over the casket. Melvin is dressed in a black shirt, blue jeans, and polished boots. He wears a black scarf, the sign of a medicine man, tied with a special knot that hangs loosely around his neck. Otherwise there is no adornment — Apache medicine men don't wear necklaces or pins.

I watch my older brother Roy as he moves through the crowd of mourners, talking and shaking hands. He's meeting new people at the same time that he's renewing old friendships. He has a camera, and now and then he pauses to take pictures. My son Michael Mithlo greets many of the mourners as they press forward, quietly and respectfully, to obtain a final glimpse of Watson Mithlo. Michael smiles as he brushes the tears from his eyes. All the brothers, sisters, and grandchildren are here to commemorate this solemn event.

I see my father lying in the coffin in front of me: in sleep, at rest, in peace. He lies on a warm Indian blanket. He wears a snap-button gray shirt, black leather vest, and blue jeans. A white Stetson hat sits on his shoulder. His feet are shod in a pair of new Nocona boots.

Melvin continues to shake pollen on Dad's body and face, which is covered with a square black cloth to hide his identity from anyone who might want to disfigure him during his long journey to the afterlife. Despite the crush of people, there's a silence inside the church, a reverent hush. Few people have ever witnessed a traditional Apache funeral. In the past, traditional funerals were held outdoors and conducted by medicine men. Few of the mourners present this day are Apaches; the majority are Choctaws, Creeks, Comanches, Kiowas, Kiowa Apaches, Caddoes, Wichitas, and Delawares. Some are even non-Indians. All are respectful and absorbed in their own thoughts and feelings.

Melvin chants and murmurs to Dad as he bends over him. He checks inside the casket to make sure that Dad has with him all the items he will need on the journey to the Creator. A black-handled knife protrudes from Dad's silver concho belt looped around his waist; the belt also holds a bag of tobacco, rolling papers, a book of matches, and a lead pencil. Around his neck hangs the silver and turquoise necklace of a Mountain Spirit dancer. Tucked in his vest is a Snickers candy bar; in his pocket there's a roll of ten one-hundred-dollar bills. In his hands he holds a pair of tan goatskin gloves and a pair of silver spurs. A black book nestles in the crook of his arm. By his side lies a Winchester rifle. He has everything with him to make his trip. Everything, that is, except for his favorite roan horse, which waits under the trees on the south side of the church, tethered to a branch with a hemp rope, grazing on a patch of grass.

The white headstone, courtesy of the U.S. Army — under which he will soon rest — reads:

> WATSON (BILL) MITHLO
>
> 1886–1993
>
> CHIRICAHUA APACHE
>
> Last P.O.W. from Castillo de San Marcos, St. Augustine, Florida
>
> Chief Chihuahua's Band

It seems fitting that Dad died on the Fourth of July, his (acknowledged) birthday. His parents had no record of his actual birthdate. They only knew he was born during the "hot days." That was approximately one hundred and seven years ago, in far-off Florida, in the Spanish colonial town of St. Augustine. He is survived by our mother; his wife, Lavina Chasenah-Mithlo; and his children: Roy Mitchell, Kenneth Chasenah, Leatrice Pewewardy-Jay, Harry Mithlo, Eugene Mithlo, Elvina Mithlo-Poolaw, Lavera Mithlo-Birdshead, Bill Mithlo, and Melvin Mithlo.

Dad died on July 4, 1993, at 5:30 p.m. while his birthday dinner was being prepared. He had taken his shower and eaten a big breakfast. In the afternoon he lay down to rest; a while later, he sat up and made a motion as if to welcome someone into the room. Mom insisted that he wasn't calling for her but for someone else whom she couldn't identify. He kept talking and making a "Come here!" motion. Then he lay down on his side and passed from this world. "Dad is gone," she said.

The old warrior lay down and died. He wasn't sick; he wasn't suffering from any specific complaint. He was worn out from having lived such a long life. The spirits entered the room, and Dad left with them.

This is the story of Watson Mithlo, Chiricahua Apache Prisoner of War, his family and his life. He lived during a time not so long ago. Long ago in numbers maybe, but not in the memory of the people who knew him. The span of his life encompassed more than a century, dating from the days when there were no cars or airplanes, no modern medicine or men walking on the moon.

Watson Mithlo's life embodies the life of the Chiricahua Apache people and the life of a Chiricahua prisoner of war. It is a story he shared with me, Harry Mithlo, when I was a youngster. I think someday he thought that I would tell the story, which I am hoping to do now in collaboration with the writer Conger Beasley Jr. It is the story of how our people came from the Chiricahua Mountains of southeast Arizona. It begins with the voice of my father telling what life was like back then.

What I tell you will be what I have been told by my father and mother and aunts, uncles, brothers, sisters, cousins, and friends. It's been given to me over the years in pieces, which I hope to put together like a mosaic, telling it the way it was told to me. The storyline may jump around, from the present to the future to the past. Indian stories do not follow a strict linear construction with a clear-cut beginning, middle, and end. Instead, everything seems to take place at the same time. All the elements of the story are caught up in a kind of ongoing, never-ending, simultaneous present. There are three main voices in this book: Watson, Harry, and Conger. Each contributes his own information and emotions. The book is a composite of our feelings and thoughts.

WATSON

There was peace and happiness among the Apaches dwelling in the mountains. I remember the clear-running streams, the abundant wildlife, the flocks of birds, the ancient cottonwoods, the leafy sycamores, the bristling pines, the shiny grass. This was the home of the Chiricahua people, and it was perfect for them until the White Eyes (Americans) came.

My father's name was Fun. He was a brave man, an intrepid warrior. Once in a firefight with the Mexicans he saved Geronimo's life. Geronimo was pinned down by an ambush and couldn't move. Fun leaped to his feet and darted back and forth toward the Mexicans, reloading his single-shot carbine with bullets clamped between his fingers, zigzagging so fast the Mexicans couldn't follow him. Each time Fun fired his rifle, a Mexican fell. On level ground, the Apache warrior knew how to bob and weave and work his weapon with amazing speed. When he attacked the enemy, he turned sideways at an angle so as to present the smallest target. He was a master of speed and evasiveness, so fast, it was said, he could see the bullets coming and dodge them.

CONGER

There is a difference between real magic and that which has been synthetically contrived. I don't know much about the Apache, but I'm looking forward to finding out. The confluence of these vectors — Watson, Harry, Conger, the Landscape, the People — is the real story; reality as a quivering mesh of multiple influences operating simultaneously throughout the cosmos, buttressed by the presence of one's own personal numinous image (Jesus Christ, Gautama Buddha, Muhammad, Geronimo) that connects and keeps them buoyant and balanced.

Anthropologists claim the Apache came from the north, the boreal forests of Canada, where the snow stacks high and bright lights flash and surge in sinuous coils across the sky. These same anthropologists say the Apache belong to the Athabascan linguistic group; their relatives, the Dene ("the People"), still live in this remote region of northwest Canada. According to the anthropologists, between AD 900 and AD 1200 something — the threat of starvation, enemies, climate change — forced the Dene to migrate south along the Front Range of the Rocky Mountains, a distance of several thousand miles, to the plains of eastern New Mexico. One of these groups eventually settled in the Four Corners region, where they became known as the Navajo. A second group called the Apache — a word in their own language meaning "enemy" — followed the buffalo as they had followed the caribou in the north, trudging on foot from place to place, carrying their entire material culture on their backs.

Harry Mithlo doesn't believe the Apache came from Canada; neither does anyone else in his family. "I don't believe what the anthropologists say," Harry grumbled. "Their problem is that they don't believe anything unless it's in a book. They won't listen to us. They don't think the stories we tell about ourselves provide enough proof as to who we are and where we came from. We say we did not come from Canada but that we emerged as a people in the Chiricahua Mountains, a gnarled and twisty maze of mountains in southeast Arizona. We say these mountains, and not Canada, is our true ancestral home."

A pained expression crept across his face. "If we came from any place else, it was from the south, from Mexico."

Divided into clan and family groups, the Chiricahua migrated around present-day Arizona and New Mexico, aided by the horse (which had been introduced by the Spanish to the region in the sixteenth century), but mostly on foot. They wintered in snug valleys nestled between jagged peaks, sheltered by brush wikiups, dome-shaped dwellings fashioned out of stick frames, insulated with bearskins and buffalo robes. The Chiricahua range offered not only a refuge but also a source of food and spiritual power. Deep in the crevices near the summits, tucked away in the shadows cast by conifer and deciduous trees, dwelt the Mountain Spirits (Gah'e), powerful deities with masked faces and trident headdresses, whom the people called upon when they needed help.

This isn't the first time that I've been chided by native people for entertaining, uncritically, the opinions and theories of the anthropologists. One time on the Pine Ridge reservation in South Dakota, I was taken to task for contending that the Lakota originated in the Great Lakes region and not in the Black Hills, which they believe was their true entry port to the upper world. It seems as if native people cannot really define themselves as a viable entity until they inhabit a specific landscape that they come to know intimately through their senses and the soles of their bare feet as they walk to wherever it is they need to go.

Harry and I were driving through the countryside around Lawton, Oklahoma, where Harry lives. It was a fine day to be out looking around—blue sky, puffy white clouds, moist air laced with the scent of fresh buffalo grass.

"Have you heard the Apache creation story?" Harry asked.

"No."

"Well, give a listen. It's got some interesting things in it."

He chuckled to himself and started in.

"The supreme deity of the Apache, the Giver of Life, is called Ussen, One story has it that Ussen cohabited with White Painted Woman and had a son named Child of the Water. At that time there were so many bad people in the world that Ussen decided to get rid of them.

A sour expression rippled across Harry's fleshy face. "Sort of like today."

He chuckled again.

"Ussen sent a flood raging across the earth to wash away the badness in the world. He made it rain for a long time. Once the rain stopped, Child of the Water and White Painted Woman got busy making babies so they could populate the world again."

I listened intently. Harry's a big man, tall, with powerful shoulders. When on his feet he stands erect, a laconic fellow who speaks in a direct, measured voice. I looked out the car window at the easy, undulating landscape of southwest Oklahoma; it was six hundred miles from here to the Chiricahua Mountains in southeast Arizona.

"One time there was a battle between the birds and the animals over darkness and light," Harry continued. "The birds wanted the cosmos to be well lit; the animals wanted it to be dark. The birds won, but only a few human beings remained alive after the battle. One of them was White Painted Woman. She gave birth to a son whom she concealed in a cave to protect him from the only beast that survived the fight: a dragon. The boy was nearly killed by the dragon, but instead he managed to slay the beast with a bow and arrow. For such a remarkable feat he was given the name 'Apache.' Tradition indicates that all Chiricahuas stem from this particular child."

What am I doing in this book, a middle-aged white guy with a hyperactive imagination? What am I doing riding around in a pickup truck with an Apache elder named Harry Mithlo? Harry wants to write a book about his father and the Chiricahua Apache. A freelance editor/writer from Kansas City, Missouri, I have been asked to assist in this endeavor. I know next to nothing about the Apache. I have come to the right source, though. Harry is a natural raconteur — savvy, funny, insightful — with a profound affection for his people.

"Warfare," he tells me, as we continue our spin through the Oklahoma countryside, "was an important activity in Apache life. The people awarded high honors to a successful warrior. To become a warrior a youth had to go on the war path with a party of warriors on at least four separate occasions, a process referred to as *dihoke*. On the first trip the boy ate sparingly. On each of the subsequent ventures, he functioned as a kind of gofer, taking care of the horses, cooking food, doing the countless little things that needed to be done. He wasn't allowed to speak to any warrior except to answer a direct question, or when told to speak. He was expected to learn the sacred name for everything used in war; once the warriors made contact with the enemy, no common names were used to identify anything. War had its own vocabulary. It was a religious undertaking."

I hear a voice in my head like Harry's, but it actually sounds more like Watson, his father. Or what I imagine Watson might sound like could I actually hear his voice. I see the book that we are collaborating on as a chorus of disembodied voices contributing to a new perspective of a people and their history.

The more time I spend with Harry the more I hear a third voice, a collective voice, composed of all the Apaches as they engage in an ongoing dialogue between themselves and the natural world—talking, remembering, questioning. It's important that that collective voice be nurtured and stroked. Part of my job is to create a reciprocity between the Chiricahua and myself wherein a kind of hope can be generated. Where I am able not only to hear what they have to say but understand it as well. To become Apache, insofar as that might be possible. It's not possible, I know, so what am I saying? I need to digest enough of their culture to give the illusion of identification. To embrace their way, at the same time to draw closer to my own.

Does this make sense? I didn't think so.

What I'm talking about is something that doesn't lend itself to facile interpretation. The Apache world is bipolar, divided into pairs of complementary halves, each half containing the same essential features; within such constraints, the Apache maintains his equilibrium by constantly monitoring where he is and why. The topical features he encounters every day reflect his identification with place; he fits inside his own skin as snugly as a foot into a familiar sock. It's important to know who you are, and one of the ways that you can gain that knowledge is to keep yourself alert and ready. Accept the world as you find it. Everything is the same, no matter where you go. "Today is a good day to die." At this level of consciousness, at this pitch of awareness, any day is a good day to die.

Let me start over. I am attracted to the Indian people because, for me, they represent the Other: an alternative to the bloated carcass of contemporary Anglo life. As Tim Giago (Lakota), founder of *Lakota Times* (1981), which then became *Indian Country Today* (1992), said to me one time, "We're not White and we're not Black. We're Indians. We are different. Not better, just different. We have our own history and stories. Above all, we have those stories about our people, where they came from. We don't want the material rewards of an industrial society, the big cars and fancy houses. We want decent housing and transportation and maybe a college education, but not at the expense of our reverence for the land, our ceremonies and rituals, our dances and the well-being of our children and elders.

"Indians help each other," Tim concluded. "They share. Even when they have nothing, they share."

HARRY

I walk in my father's footsteps along the Chiricahua pathways in Arizona, on land that our people knew and cherished. I can understand why this place was paradise to the Chiricahua. I walk in the tall grass near a brook and see footprints in the sand left by the animals that come here to drink.

The grassy slopes between the mountains are so vast one can travel across them and see from one horizon to the next. In my father's day, Apaches could look at the smooth, rippling terrain between the peaks and know if someone was traveling toward them or running away. They knew every landmark as they knew the features of their bodies.

The sun bears down on my neck and shoulders. Puffy clouds float by, casting shadows as they pass. The shade thrown down by these clouds offers little relief from the heat.

The Chiricahua could never be sure what was hidden in those crevices and arroyos that creased the earth between the foothills. There could be snakes, cougars, enemies. The Apache are wary of rattlesnakes; the reptiles are capable of inflicting serious injury to a rider or his horse. Their venom can cause instant death. We respect them; at the same time we make sure there is plenty of distance between us.

Rattlesnakes teach us to be attentive, to acknowledge and understand that danger is always with us. Rattlesnakes teach us about the necessity of keeping our thoughts and emotions steady and alert. Wherever we go, there is danger. We must see it before it sees us.

The grassy slopes between the mountain ranges are covered with light-colored yucca, brush mesquite, tufts of sage, and sunburned grasses. We used these features as landmarks when we traveled from place to place. We could look at the peaks and mountains and locate the places where food and ammunition were cached, where fresh water could be found.

When the clouds piled up in dark thunderheads, especially in late summer, we knew that rain was on the way. Rain on the grassy uplands meant water for the wildlife and fresh drinking water for the Chiricahua.

Some places in the Chiricahua Mountains are devoid of trees and grass. The mountains rise sharply, showing the stretch marks of their slow, painful growth. The rocks are granite, and they have jagged edges. The pattern of erosion has sculpted them into fantastic shapes and figures. It is impossible to imagine you are alone when you walk the trails that wind through this rugged confluence of peaks and cliffs. The spirits are everywhere.

High in the foothills, the air is full of the scent of cedar and pine. It is cooler and greener among the red oaks and the tall agave plants. The clouds swell and puff; thunder rumbles in the distance.

Boulders crown the tops of the peaks that push up through the heart of the Chiricahua Mountains. I am happy to be here; I feel close to the spirits of my ancestors. I am looking at the same features they once saw. The smell of cedar and pine reminds me of a campsite with wickiups and open fires. I smell fresh meat cooking over a bed of smoldering coals. I hear dogs barking. All the everyday sounds of a traditional Apache encampment can be heard at the spot where I now sit on a rock in the shade of a pine tree in the heart of the Chiricahua Mountains.

My family was here long before they were sent to Florida as prisoners of war. They belonged to Chief Chihuahua's band of Chiricahua Apaches. This part of Arizona is the place where Ussen, our Creator, put us. We have always lived here and nowhere else. We like it. Some people don't, but we do. The barren landscape makes us resourceful; we are better fighters because of it. We know which plants are harmful and which are not. It's not easy living in the desert. The White Eyes hated it. To the Apache, it was home. It had everything they needed.

WATSON

I hear the ancient songs of my ancestors and see the figures of the Mountain Spirit dancers. The Mountain Spirit Dance is a deeply emotional dance given by my people to cure illness and pay homage to the natural world. The presence of the Mountain Spirit dancers has sustained me throughout the one hundred years of my life.

HARRY

On the edge of the rural hamlet of Apache, Oklahoma, there's a grassy circle where, once a year — the first weekend in October — the dances are performed. These are not ordinary dances; they are deeply spiritual. They connect us with our ancestors and loved ones. They renew our strength for the difficulties ahead.

At the center of the dance circle, starting at sundown, a big fire burns fiercely, around which the dancers bob and weave, touching the ground with the tips of their magic wands: touching, connecting, replenishing.

When a person died, it was the Apache custom to remove all traces of his or her identity, including their name. It's as if they didn't exist. People told stories about adventures and encampments, raids and disasters; they never uttered the names of the deceased, even though the memory of who they were remained very much in our hearts. I know my father's name and I will speak it here because I was born in a different time and have been brought up among white people and have assimilated many of their customs.

WATSON

We wandered the land in rhythm to our own sense of time. We did not have clocks or calendars; instead, we kept track of time, not in years that we could add and subtract, but by the winters we could remember, the enemies we attacked, those who attacked us, the stories we told about them. We tracked time by the passage of the sun and the moon and the stars. We tracked time by the flow of the wind, by the migration of birds. Our stories told of a cold and rainy time, a hot and dry time, a time when the leaves changed colors, a time when the grass turned green.

We had no months or years to remember or names from the past we had to recall. We lived in the present, the steady, beckoning Now, and our stories jumped back and forth in a way that enabled us to avoid mentioning the names of the dead; certain events were never mentioned, and we have many warriors from the past who remain unknown to us except in spirit.

The Mexicans came to our land from the south before the arrival of the White Eyes. We fought the Mexicans and raided deep into their country. We raided their houses for food and ammunition, anything to keep us going. Sometimes we were peaceful and visited them like friends, eating with them and sleeping in their houses like family.

The White Eyes were different. We fought with them constantly. We were never able to let down our guard when we were in their presence. They weren't content with taking a portion of what we had; they wanted it all. We were careful not to call attention to ourselves by lighting fires or riding out on the open plains during the day when our dust could be sighted.

Apache warriors were always eager to fight the White Eyes. They killed our wildlife and stole our homeland, and we hated them. Fighting was a way of life for us. We never killed or harmed anyone unless they resisted or tried to harm us. We never killed or violated women during our raids. We never took the scalp of the enemy we fought.

The U.S. Army pursued the Apache, but they could not keep up with us. We moved too fast. We knew how to disappear into the bush. War leaders like Geronimo possessed the ability to manipulate the flow of ordinary time, to slow it down or speed it up. To keep up with us, the Army was forced to hire San Carlos Apaches and White Mountain Apaches to track us down and bring us into captivity. The White Mountain Apaches hated the Chiricahua Apaches, and we hated them back with the fiercest kind of hatred.

CONGER

I come from a culture that believes that nothing is valid unless it has been recorded or written down. At school I loved reading about history and people, who they were and why they did what they did. But that's not the only means by which vital information is transmitted; there are other kinds of communication, colloquial and spoken, rather than printed upon a sheet of paper or projected upon a screen. Listening to Harry and his family tell stories about the Chiricahua enables me to tap into a direct line between them and the events that shaped their lives. Harry is making me aware of another facet of learning: an oral tradition, spoken rather than written, where there is no past or future, only the present, the ongoing Now.

In my culture we might describe it as the ultimate existential moment, fluid enough to encompass a world of contrasting particulars, selective enough to single out those factors that are most important to the well-being of the people. The ability to keep on going and doing, the ability to embrace contrary elements in the same deep breath, the ability to maintain faith and hope in a hostile world.

Harry Mithlo is a full-blood Indian, half Apache, half Comanche. He was educated (for the most part) in the white man's schools. He comes from two cultures. He can see (when he has to) from both perspectives. He has a foot in both camps. I envy him. I think the more perspectives you have to see things with, the better chance you have of becoming a genuine person in the world.

It goes deeper than that. I will never know Harry as thoroughly as I might like. He is an Indian; I am an Anglo. At the core of both of us there is an opacity that defies analysis, a reluctance to believe that human beings can actually behave in a mutually satisfying fashion. We are both, Anglo and Indian, hopelessly isolated. Things for me need to be footnoted properly. I need to know their source, where they come from. Just because I feel intensely about something doesn't necessarily mean I understand what that something means. It's an odd kind of bond to be shackled with; it seems so promising, while at the same time it's so difficult to achieve. Show me the proper credentials and I will believe anything you say. But how do we verify the primacy of events through the flimsy medium of story? A lone voice barking in the dark, a fragile narrative, spun out by a solitary speaker with a spider's fluency.

Anglo culture craves exactness and precision, solidity and single-mindedness.

Proof.

From the 1850s to the 1880s, the Chiricahua were called upon to defend their precarious hold on the mountains of southeast Arizona. In 1859, the Butterfield Overland Stage Company ran its wagons through Apache Pass, hauling mail and passengers between the Texas frontier and California. As long as the traffic was minimal, an uneasy peace prevailed; sporadic clashes occurred, the occasional ambush, but a full-scale war was averted.

In 1861, a company of mounted infantry entered Apache Pass from the west. A young officer, Lieutenant George S. Bascom, in a face-to-face confrontation, accused Chiricahua war chief Cochise of child abduction and cattle thievery. Cochise denied the accusations. Bascom stood his ground. Fighting broke out; with its dense groves and rocky slopes, Apache Pass was a perfect place to bushwhack an unsuspecting enemy.

The volatile situation called for patience and experience, neither of which Bascom possessed. After finding the bodies of three mutilated Americans, he ordered the hanging of six Apache hostages. Cochise and his stalwarts vowed revenge. The petty thievery they had previously engaged in escalated into all-out war. From this point on the two sides tore into one another with ruthless ferocity.

Apache Pass became the focal point of the worsening conflict; it badly needed a permanent military presence to calm things down. In July 1862, Fort Bowie was established at the top of the pass, a short distance from the vital springs, possession of which in the Arizona heat meant the difference between survival and death. The fort was effective; the Chiricahua never again controlled Apache Pass.

Beginning in the 1860s, a procession of military figures appeared and disappeared through the revolving door of U.S. Army command in southeast Arizona. The Army sent their best senior and junior officers to deal with the elusive Chiricahua—Generals James Carleton, George Crook, Oliver Otis Howard, and Nelson Miles; Captains Charles Gatewood, John G. Bourke, Emmet Crawford, and Witt Davis; Lieutenants Henry Lawton and Leonard Wood, leading a contingent of tough, resilient, first-rate mounted troops.

Likewise, as much as any Indian faction in North America, the Chiricahua were blessed with exceptional leaders. Their names form an illustrious roster: Victorio, Cochise, Nana, Natchez, Mangas Coloradas, Chatto, Geronimo, Chihuahua. Says historian Robert Utley, "In all the wars for the North American continent, the European invader encountered no more formidable adversary than the Apache warrior."

The Army finally managed to corral the Chiricahua by outright deception. Chasing them down was a hopeless task; by the 1880s, they were probably the finest desert warriors in the world. Their endurance was astounding. They were indefatigable. They had an uncanny ability to blend into the terrain. They knew how to live off the land. They appeared and disappeared with effortless ease.

In September 1886, Geronimo and the other Chiricahua leaders met General George Crook in a conference at Skeleton Canyon (*Cañon de los Embudos*)—a lava bed spilling over the top of a conical hill, surrounded by deep ravines, a few miles from the Mexican border. The Indians agreed to lay down their arms on condition that they and their families would be confined somewhere on the Atlantic coast for no longer than two years, after which they would return to their beloved mountains and Apache Pass.

As fate would have it, with the compromise agreed upon by both sides, the night after this decisive parley Geronimo met up with an unscrupulous whisky dealer who sold him a batch of tiswin (fermented beer). Much to the dismay of the Blue Coats, the Chiricahua went on a toot; twenty men, thirteen women, and two children, accompanied by the Warrior Geronimo, stole out of camp the next day and disappeared into the Sierra Madre Mountains of northern Mexico.

Back in Washington, the commander of the U.S. Army, Lieutenant General Philip Sheridan, exploded with bitter wrath. In no uncertain terms he ordered General Crook, who had engineered the compromise, to demand the unconditional surrender of the Indians, or else they were to be "destroyed."

Sheridan was weary of failure; every time his troopers appeared on the verge of bottling up the Chiricahua, they managed to slip away. This had gone on for years, and it was humiliating. The politicos in Washington were starting to point fingers and name names.

Crook was devastated; the many years of dedicated effort to bring the Apache to bay disappeared in a blink. Smarting under the rebuke from his senior officer, he resigned his command. The next day Sheridan appointed a new leader to the Department of Arizona, a vain, conceited, ambitious brigadier general named Nelson A. Miles. The first thing Miles did was to beef up the string of border outposts that provided a porous line of defense against Apache attack across the border from Mexico. He also discharged the majority of the Apache scouts, preferring to utilize regular veterans so as not to have to share the glory when the time came (and it would come) for the Chiricahua to stop fighting.

Miles then planned a new offensive into Mexico, led by an elite column of troopers, who pushed all the way into the Yaqui River country of northern Sonora. For four grueling months, the column pursued the Apaches, toiling over one dreary, back-cracking mountain after another. At one point, it was estimated that some 5,000 soldiers—nearly one quarter of the total complement of American Army personnel nationwide—were employed in the effort to chase down thirty-eight Chiricahua men, women, and children. Miles also made extensive use of a glass device called the heliograph, consisting of mirrors mounted on a tripod that in the hands of a skilled operator could catch the sun's rays and flash messages from mountaintop to mountaintop, forty to fifty miles apart.

Miles was convinced that success against the Apache depended upon moving those Chiricahua already ensconced on Arizona reservations totally out of the territory. On September 7, 1886—in a stunning move that contradicted everything they had been promised—Army units on the Fort Apache reservation rounded up 382 Chiricahua men, women, and children, including virtually all the remaining scouts who had loyally served the Army, and under close watch marched them to the railroad town of Holbrook, Arizona Territory, about ninety miles away.

Geronimo objected strenuously. He was tired of running and wanted to settle down on territory that belonged indisputably to the Chiricahua. He was not the easiest adversary to appease. By this time his own people, who claimed he was a liar and a blowhard, distrusted him. Perhaps he thought that by behaving in a petulant manner he might cut a better deal for his people. "Take us to the reservation," he growled at the Blue Coats, "or we'll finish the fight right here."

That's when he was told that there were no Chiricahua left at the Fort Apache Reservation. All the kinfolk had been rounded up, put on trains, and sent to Florida. General Miles made it perfectly clear: If Geronimo wanted to see his family again, he had to agree to the Army's terms; otherwise, he and the other members of the band would be forced to live in the midst of other Apache groups, many of whom hated the Chiricahua.

WATSON

My mother's name was Tah-Tzil-Toey. She told me that the soldiers held Chief Chihuahua and our band in a warehouse at Fort Bowie for four days after they laid down their weapons. The soldiers questioned him closely. They wouldn't let him eat or drink, and they beat him. Several days later, he was released back to the people. He was very weak when he returned. His body was covered with welts and bruises.

We rode in wagons from Fort Bowie, Arizona Territory, to a railroad station about twenty miles away. Chief Chihuahua and his band were the first to go. The warriors were shackled in chains. We didn't know where we were going. We knew the soldiers wanted to kill us. We knew they wanted to abuse our women. We watched every move they made. We remained stone-faced and impassive; we couldn't let them know our real feelings. The Blue Coats had food for us, but they wouldn't hand it out. We were always hungry.

Worst of all was to watch the children suffer, their empty bellies cramped with pain. We gave them leather scraps they could chew on and pretend they were eating something. The Army had food, but they wouldn't give it out. The children sat very still, their dark eyes brimming with tears. They did not cry. Apache children are trained from birth never to cry. Their parents told them that if they cried, the soldiers would kill them.

The day we left Fort Bowie we looked long and hard at the mountains. We realized that we were leaving the land that we loved. The mountains gave us everything we needed: food, clothing, shelter. Later, when we were in prison in Florida, my mother's eyes welled with tears whenever she mentioned the Chiricahua Mountains.

I am speaking to you from my mother's womb. I am safe here, while she must suffer the pain of captivity. But she is strong, and will not give in. Each new Chiricahua generation must come to terms with this terrible event.

My aunt Tsis-tohn rode with a band of Apaches who fought the U.S. Army to avoid being captured or killed. One day she slipped back into Fort Apache to visit her mother. Tsis-tohn's mother did not want Tsis-tohn to bear a child while the Apaches were at war. She didn't want her to be a burden to the warriors. Tsis-tohn's mother made a special medicine to prevent her from getting pregnant. The medicine worked. My aunt Tsis-tohn never bore a child in her lifetime.

Apache women such as Tsis-tohn frequently distinguished themselves in battle. Their toughness and resilience enabled them to perform amazing feats.

Gouyen (her name means "Wise Woman") was born in the area known as Gran Apachería around 1857. In 1879, a war party of Comanches raided her village, killing her husband. Sick with rage, she went off into the night, wearing her puberty ceremony buckskin dress, carrying a water jug and some dried meat. As a young girl she had received warrior training, which she now put to use, following the Comanche across the desert on foot for four nights until she came upon their camp.

Concealed in the shadows, she spied her husband's scalp tied to the belt of a Comanche war chief. She slipped into the circle of dancers celebrating their successful raid and began flirting with the chief. He stumbled drunkenly as she lured him away from the circle; outside in the darkness, she plunged a black-handled knife into his stomach and ripped out his guts. For good measure she scalped him. Taking his breechclout and moccasins, she stole a horse and galloped for two days back to the Apache camp, where she collapsed into the arms of her family, her puberty dress smeared with the Comanche warrior's blood.

Aunt Tsis-tohn told us how the soldiers and the Apache scouts rounded up the other Chiricahua Apaches at Fort Apache, Arizona Territory. This happened in August 1886. A few Apache bands stayed near the fort to receive food, blankets, and cooking utensils. Food consisted of coffee, sugar, flour, dried beans, and a little beef. Small bands of Chiricahuas stole into the camps of their relatives at night. The relatives gave them supplies and the latest information. The warriors rode off into the dark before anyone realized they were there.

We were good at that — creeping and skulking. We knew how to mix and merge. We knew how to make ourselves invisible, even when burdened with livestock, infants, and old folks. No one really knew who we were or where we came from. We could erase the features from our faces, and hang them in a tree where they were indistinguishable from the leaves. We took great solace in knowing that, no matter how hard they tried, few outsiders would ever understand us. We remain that way today. Defiant and inscrutable.

One day we were told to form a line at midday in the hot sun. We thought we were going to receive our rations. Instead of rations, they lined us up and took our weapons, including the knives we used to cut our meat with. It was a very bad day. Every Apache was taken prisoner, whether he had fought with the Blue Coats or not. It was a terrible experience; the women, children, and old people were half-crazy with fear.

The soldiers shackled the warriors' legs, cuffed their wrists with locks and chains, and loaded them into wagons. A warrior named Zele was handcuffed with steel bands that locked around his wrists and ankles. He couldn't raise his arms over his head, and he could only take small steps. The locks pinched his arms and legs; the chains rattled and clinked whenever he made the slightest move.

The wagons left Fort Apache when the sun was high, heading north toward Holbrook, Arizona Territory, ninety miles away. They were followed by women and children on foot, trailing in ragged columns behind the wagons. Some women tried to slip into the bush so they could circle back to their camps, but the soldiers maintained a tight guard.

The route from Fort Apache to Holbrook was difficult, but it was familiar to us because we had been there before. The terrain was part desert and part forest. The wagon train bumped and rattled through deep gorges between steep, rocky walls. It went up and down through dense brush and forest, across streams and rivers. The weather was hot. Day and night for nearly a week we wore the same clothes; we had no chance to wash. There was never enough to eat. The way to Holbrook was long and difficult. The trail snaked through deep ravines, following narrow forest paths. Tall pines with a fragrant orange bark provided some relief; hill after hill, dotted with sagebrush, rolled endlessly to the horizon. The march was especially difficult for the women and children. Many were barefoot. The sharp rocks cut their feet.

The soldiers shot several cows. Apache women and children collected firewood. The women butchered the livestock and cooked the meat. Soldiers stood nearby, hands on their hips, laughing and watching. We knew they wanted to kill us. How much easier we would be to deal with if we were dead! Alive, we might escape and attack them in the middle of the night. They were fearful that we would mutilate them after they were dead. Stories about what the Apache did to the dead and wounded White Eyes were greatly exaggerated. If we carved them up, it was only after they were dead. We believed the condition a cadaver was left in carried through to the afterlife. This did not become a factor until the treacherous General Carleton lured Chief Mangas Coloradas into his camp under a flag of truce, promising him protection, then killing him. The soldiers cut off his head and boiled the flesh and hair off his skull. The great chief had to go headless through the afterlife.

We didn't have time to collect our personal effects at Fort Apache when the soldiers rounded us up. We had to leave everything behind, including our horses, cattle, and dogs. All the dogs — and there were hundreds of them — followed us, howling and whining. The soldiers kept the warriors shackled at all times to prevent them from trying to join the dogs outside.

The weather turned cool; rain drizzled down. The women held the children to their bodies to keep them warm as they walked behind the wagons. It wasn't any better riding in the wagons, bouncing over the rough trails. The soldiers and the Apache scouts stood guard over us 'round the clock. Enveloped by clouds of flies, the commissary cattle, herded by the Apache scouts, tramped behind the Apache prisoners.

We saw Holbrook to the north one afternoon as we passed over a low hill. Two hours later the wagons creaked to a halt. We camped near the station that night; we did not know that it was the last night we would ever spend in our homeland. After dark, the older men sang Apache songs. The songs soothed us and gave us strength.

The next day we were told that we were going to Florida. We had never heard of Florida. We had no idea where it was. We were told that we would be there for no more than two years, and then we would be free to come back to Arizona. How far was Florida from Arizona? We didn't know. The White Eyes had lied to us before, and no doubt they were lying to us again. A few of the soldiers tried to reassure our leaders that Florida was a lot like Arizona, and we would be comfortable there.

We didn't sleep that night, knowing in the morning we'd be put on a train and sent on our way to Florida. The soldiers woke us early so we could eat something. The children were difficult to control. We could see the train chugging toward us in the distance, showers of cinders and sparks belching from its smokestack.

The locomotive screeched to a halt, blowing out clouds of steam. The children began to scream and cry. They must have sensed what was about to happen. Old men and women fell to the ground in fits of terror. Many had never seen a locomotive before, and the noise it made with steam boiling out of the engine terrified them.

Where were we going? How long would it take? What would happen to us when we got there?

The steam continued to blow out between the big iron wheels with a piercing shriek. The women and children continued to bawl and cry as the soldiers and scouts lifted them up into the cars. Only a few of us had ever been on a train before, or even been this close to one.

The interior of the train was gloomy, the windows covered with dark cloth. We were told to sit with our backs to each other. When the last person was jammed into the car, the soldiers closed the doors; a guard was posted at each door. It was then that the hand and leg irons were removed from the feet and arms of the warriors. The hot morning sun, the press of bodies against one another, made us uncomfortable; sweat dripped down our backs and arms.

The dogs followed the steel tracks for miles after the train pulled out of Holbrook. They yelped and howled as if they knew they would never see us again. The sound was sad and mournful; it stayed in our hearts for a long time. Hundreds of dogs, snarling and snapping, tried frantically to keep abreast of the moving cars. There wasn't room for all of them to run; half of them would lie on the ground while the other half trampled them. Gradually they thinned out as the train gathered speed, but a few of them kept going for twenty miles or more until they dropped from exhaustion. Later that day, the local residents and cow-punchers had great sport with the dogs, shooting them from the saddle, leaving their carcasses to rot in the sun.

Once seated, we were not permitted to move about or leave the car. Not all the Apache people who were taken prisoner that day knew each other. It was an awkward situation. We took heart from the fact that a few of the Chiricahuas were still free in the mountains, fighting the White Eyes. We took heart in the fact that the warrior Geronimo never officially surrendered to the U.S. government. He was never defeated in battle by the Blue Coats; he finally agreed to come in because all his people had been captured, and he missed his family and homeland. An Apache scout told him, "All of the Chiricahua people have been captured, and you are the only one left."

We sat and waited for time to pass. The soldiers were afraid that the warriors would try to escape, so they watched us carefully.

Two warriors, Massai and Gray Lizard, did escape. Massai was an Apache, Gray Lizard a Tonkawa. When the guards looked the other way, they worked the bars loose on the window next to where they sat. Somewhere in the Missouri Ozarks, as the train toiled up a long slope, they took advantage of the slow speed to wiggle through the bars and jump to the ground.

Massai's wife was on the train; she knew she couldn't leave because of the children, but she urged Massai and Gray Lizard to escape. She gave them her food so they would have something to eat. On the ground at last, they ran through the forest as fast as they could. After many adventures, they made their way back to New Mexico. When they saw the White Mountain on the Mescalero Apache Reservation, they knew they were close to home. They arrived back in Apache country in the fall of 1887.

The train banged and rattled, making a fearful racket. The story is everything.

Twice a day the Apache soldiers brought us food. They liked to taunt us, saying that the White Eyes intended to chop off our heads when we reached Florida. We were fearful that the soldiers would poison us, but we were so hungry we ate what they gave us. We drank water from a bucket with a single dipper. We didn't know if we would ever see our families again, so certain were we that we were going to be killed.

The train stopped at shabby little towns in the middle of nowhere for a few minutes, and then with a toot and a whistle and a blast of steam it started rolling again. At each of the stops, the White Eyes crowded against the windows with their hands cupped around their eyes, looking through the glass to catch a glimpse of the fearsome Apache. It was understandable that they wanted to see us, especially when they found out that the warrior Geronimo was among the passengers. With all the scrutiny and rubbernecking, we couldn't help but feel like animals in a zoo. Every little town was packed with people with pasty white faces, so many in fact they were like ants on a dirt trail. If you place a stick across the trail, the stick would stop them for a while, but they soon found a way around the stick to the other side. There were so many of them, and so few of us.

CONGER

There's a photograph taken somewhere in Texas of a group of Chiricahua Apaches sitting on a grassy slope at the foot of a railway embankment, just below the steel wheels of a gigantic locomotive. Geronimo is in the photo, along with Nana, Naiche, Loco, Fun (Watson Mithlo's father), and Warrior Woman Lozen. They stare impassively at the camera with stolid expressions, hands clasped in front of them or primly cupped around their knees. Several Blue Coats, clutching rifles, stand grinning on the platforms between the cars, enjoying a chuckle at the expense of the Indians who seem confused and dislocated.

I don't know where the place is exactly, somewhere outside of San Antonio, but that doesn't matter. What matters is the stony expression on the faces of the captives; Geronimo's eyes look like chiseled agates.

There's more to the photo than that. I think Watson and Harry would agree. Yes, the Apache look exhausted and spent, but they've not been defeated, only momentarily subdued. Beneath the bewilderment and confusion there's a look of sheer, indomitable power, an expression of utter defiance and resolve. They may at this moment be under armed guard, but who knows what the situation might be like a few minutes from now?

With this photo, which was widely reproduced in newspapers around the nation, the Apache became part of a new global awareness, the embodiment of a wildness and freedom that was about to undergo a profound transformation. Some people would say that the Apache were poised on the brink of becoming a remnant of a "vanished" way of life.

But the Apache aren't on the verge of vanishing; they are still here, as the photo indicates: strong, resilient, durable. The man who took the photo tried to make us think that he was witnessing the demise of an entire category of human being. The year was 1886, and the world was undergoing a radical change. Yes, the White Eyes were on the verge of powering their way around the globe, plucking up native cultures such as the Chiricahua from remote locations where they had flourished for hundreds of years and reworking them into their own messy, complicated image. The people pictured here seem an inevitable part of the landscape, as real and organic and lasting as the grass and dirt on which they sit.

Something is going on here. Circa 1886, all men everywhere, in big cities and small towns, were in the process of becoming something other than what they once were. The Apache were being called upon to relinquish traditional attitudes and practices that had enabled them to survive for a long time. The industrial grid woven by the mighty American manufacturing machine was in the process of binding the world into a tight-knit web. In place of expansive circles in which anything fit, the order of the day was to cram everything into compact boxes with right-angled corners so they could be properly counted and labeled. The world was shrinking to a finite, measurable dimension, and nobody could do anything about it. Those like the Chiricahua who were once free were on the verge of a profound change. Something would be lost forever to the world with the incarceration of these people in the Spanish dungeons of Florida.

As it appears to me in my mind: the night has put a chill into the air, and somebody has draped a blanket across Watson's knees. The fire in the hearth has dwindled to a spotty glow. Nobody knows how old Watson is. Harry knows, but he's not telling; neither is Melvin. Watson from the pouch of his mother's womb listens to what's happening out there in the world he is soon to be a part of. The upper world. He belongs there, in that world, and is ready to emerge, to show up, to take his place among his brothers and sisters in their struggle to survive as a people. He is Chiricahua. He wants to help. He presses his cheek against the umbilical cord that tethers him to his mother. It won't be long now, he thinks.

Watson's voice is low and raspy. The thick lenses of his glasses magnify the black orbs of his eyes. He is blind in one eye, the result of an accident when he was a young man, but he can see just fine out of the other. He looks around the room. People have crowded in to hear the old man talk. His stories connect them with their tumultuous past, their history, how they came to be. The stories spin from his mouth, leaving a chalky white trail arcing through the murky air.

WATSON

I can't remember how many days and nights we traveled before the train stopped long enough for us to transfer to another train. This train ride was one of the most terrible things we had to suffer. The windows were sealed and there was no fresh air. Smelly fumes from the engine seeped into the cars, nauseating the passengers and making them vomit. The soldiers treated us like cattle penned in a corral. They pushed and shoved us around to make us sit where they could see us. They yelled and screamed in a language we didn't understand. Their faces were clenched with hatred and contempt.

There was no place or privacy to urinate or defecate. Mothers held up a blanket to cover their children when they eliminated on the floor. Women held out their dresses to the sides of their legs to hide children and other women. All bodily functions took place in this car. We slept, ate, and evacuated in the same place, day after day. The stench was unbearable.

At night, the soldiers put the seats down to make a flat surface we could sleep on. We had plenty of time to think about our trip, and we could feel the jerk of the car as the train pitched forward. We worried about the horses that we had left at Fort Apache. What would happen to them? Would they be taken by the Army? Would the townspeople run them off or kill them?

And the dogs? What about them?

When we changed trains again, the soldiers with their guns and bayonets stayed with us. As we walked from one car to another, we could see blue skies. The air was sticky and humid. The weather in Arizona wasn't like this; this was like being in a sweat lodge without the heated rocks to cleanse our bodies and spirits. That heat we could tolerate; we came out of the lodge purified and replenished. This heat made us feel like we were drowning.

As we walked between the train platforms, we saw more white people standing on tiptoe, craning their necks to get a glimpse of us. They looked at us, and we looked at them. I don't know how many times we changed trains, maybe three times. In St. Augustine after we finally arrived, we walked from the train station to Fort Marion in a torchlit procession accompanied by sentries with guns. People packed the streets to gaze at us. The weather was hot and sticky and our filthy clothes clung to our foul, sweaty bodies.

It was good to get off the train and walk the earth again. The sun was bright, and it was a welcome relief to see green plants and trees and breathe fresh air. Chief Chihuahua met us at the station when we arrived in St. Augustine, Florida, on September 20, 1886. We were the second group of Apaches to arrive in Florida. We told Chief Chihuahua about the long march from Fort Bowie to Holbrook, how the warriors had been handcuffed and put in wagons, how we suffered on the train, the lack of food, the lack of sanitary facilities. Many of our people did not have enough clothing to cover themselves. The children's arms and legs were splotched with bites and sores. They were hungry. But they never complained.

As soon as we arrived, in the sultry tropical city of St. Augustine, Florida, the warriors were separated from the women and children and sent to Fort Pickens in Pensacola, Florida, over 300 miles to the west. That first night the rest of us were herded into a ragged line and forced to march by torchlight through the streets of St. Augustine, past a gallery of gawking onlookers, to our new quarters at Castillo de San Marcos (Fort Marion). A few days later, several men belonging to

Chief Chihuahua's band were put in a boat and taken across the water to Anastasia Island, an offshore barrier island with a lighthouse, where they were left to fend for themselves. The soldiers knew the island was too far from land for the Apaches to try to escape. None of them knew how to swim. Once a week a boat delivered food and tobacco, fishing equipment, oil and matches.

What were the Blue Coats thinking? We were mountain people, hunters and gatherers; we understood nothing about catching fish and eating them. We had many taboos against creatures who live in water.

Those prisoners were forced to stay on the island for many weeks. The insects made their lives unbearable. They bit and stung them night and day. We did not know who the creatures were that swarmed over the sand and swam in the sea. The crabs were frightening to look at. Apaches never ate anything that lived in the water.

The old people became confused. They would look out across the water on a windy day and think the waves rolling to shore were like clumps of foamy grass. The spectacle frightened them, and they would try to run across the water and had to be pulled back to solid ground before they drowned.

Fort Marion and the mainland were off in the distance, too far to swim to (we didn't know how to swim, anyway). Our people had never seen this much water. Many of them became queasy watching the waves rise and fall.

Several people died on the train during the long, jolting ride from Arizona to Florida. They gave up and let go of their lives. We had to leave their bodies behind, and we weren't able to properly honor them. The soldiers thought our condition was funny; they laughed and made cruel jokes. Many of us were still wearing the same clothing we had worn when we left Fort Apache.

CONGER

A faint smile wrinkles Watson's grim face. He can be stern but he can also be mirthful. I watch him carefully. He sits in the chair with his fingers intertwined, gazing up at the ceiling.

I took acid a few times in the 1960s and had at least one memorable experience. A buddy of mine named Darrell DeVore and I each popped a little, round, innocuous-looking pill the size of an aspirin that he called "White Lightning." He carried the pills, plus a stash of Oaxacan reefer, in a leather bag slung around his shoulder. Then we sat around waiting for something to happen.

Darrell and I went back all the way to first grade. If I freaked out on the acid he was there for me. He was a jazz musician and had access to just about anything he wanted in the way of psychedelics or amphetamines. He had dropped acid before. I had not.

It took a half hour for the jolt to reach my extremities, which it did with a furious rush. An hour later, it felt as if a monster gorilla the size of King Kong was clutching my back with his powerful arms, hell-bent on squeezing the marrow out of my bones. I was beset by a jittery fit. My body felt like a brown paper bag that had been wadded up and tossed in the trash. Walking carefully, I went into the downstairs bathroom, the walls of which my wife had decorated with a tranquil light-green paper featuring eighteenth-century figures in powdered wigs and knee breeches and silk cravats gamboling across a manicured lawn. I glanced into the bathroom mirror and recoiled in shock. I couldn't believe what I saw. My face was grotesque. My nose had melted across my cheeks like a pancake. My eyes jiggled in their gaping sockets like loose coins. My skin was a slur of lurid colors that made me recoil in alarm. Darrell knocked at the door. I opened it with tears in my eyes. "Don't look at yourself," he advised. "This," he said, pointing to my gruesome image in the mirror, "is just a phase you have to go through in order to reach Nirvana."

He cackled. His eyes were astonishing, blue as a pristine lagoon. Transparent as a windowpane, roomy as a walk-in closet. My feverish brain was dogged by hallucinations. At one point I found myself prowling the carpet of the living room floor, testing the weight of the twin .44 Colt revolvers strapped to my hips in leather holsters. Directly ahead of me loomed another wall decorated with paintings and tapestries. A portly man stepped out of the side door of a saloon, waving a shotgun. I dropped to one knee, pulling the revolver from its leather holster in the same smooth motion and firing at the figure before he could bring the shotgun into play. The holster was empty. There was no revolver. The fore and index fingers of my right hand served as the gun barrel. When I pulled the trigger, instead of bullets, splots of blood spurted from my fingertips and splashed against the wall, leaving no mark or stain. The sense of release was exhilarating. I fired again, drilling him in the center of the forehead. His hat, a scruffy derby with a well-worn brim, flew off. He crumpled to his knees. BAM! POW! BANG! Blood doused everything in the room: chairs, tables, a polished credenza, an old armoire, a footstool topped with a velvet pillow. And then I went postal and began firing at the ordinary objects in the room: vases, chairs, pillows, ashtrays. BAM! POW! BANG! Turning, like a ballet dancer, squeezing off shots that left red streaks hanging like bunting in the sedate air. Merely by giving my fingers a shake, I triggered a spate of deep-red bolts that shot out the barrel of my finger like tiny red tomatoes, spattering the walls and windows, but leaving no stain or mark. I fired those pistols 'til the hammers clicked apologetically. Mad, raucous, jittery. BAM! BAM! BAM!

In the kitchen, we tore through the refrigerator, looking for something to eat. Lovely chemical, that LSD. Exciting, fun, armed with warheads, with nothing to ground or connect them. Such were our synthetic visions in the 1960s. Lurid, noisy, cinematic. Cartoon displays, unattached to anyone or anything. Meaningless trips to nowhere.

I pulled the books out of another waxy-colored bookcase and tried to crawl onto the shelf and settle in for a nap, but there wasn't enough room between the shelves to lie down on, and I had to be content with flopping around the carpet like a bony carp.

WATSON

My aunt Tsis-tohn says the first time the Apache women saw a black woman they thought she was a bear! This was at Fort Marion, in St. Augustine, Florida. The woman was short and heavy, and she walked with a clumsy step.

We Apache are wary of bears. We give them great distance and never harm them. We never eat them. The black (bear) woman stood next to a cooking pot. The Apache women watched her curiously. She put a hand in the front pocket of her dress and took out something and dropped it into the pot. Then she pulled the object out of the pot and passed it back and forth between her hands. Then she stuck it in her mouth, chewed, and swallowed it!

The black woman was there to show the Apache women how to wash their clothing in a vat of boiling water. The object the black woman dropped into the pot was an egg. She boiled the egg in hot water and ate it. The Apache women were afraid that she was a bear and that she was going to cook them and eat them too!

CONGER

It's a different place in my head that I'm tending toward now. I'm outdoors somewhere on the Fort Sill reservation with Harry and his brother Eugene. I'm lying in the grass, chewing idly on a green stalk. The undulant surface of the Apache cemetery is dotted with tombstones, many bearing the remains of members of the Mithlo family.

"Watson is not buried here," said Harry. "He lies in a gravesite located near the circle of the Mountain Spirits dance pavilion on the outskirts of Apache, Oklahoma. This space is sacred. Many dances have been given here, many more to come. The dance group belongs to the Mithlo family; they're the present keepers of the regalia, headdresses, and other items pertaining to the Mountain Spirit Dance."

WATSON

As children, we played many games. One of the most important was the hoop-and-pole game. Adults also played it, betting heavily on the outcome. (Apaches are inveterate gamblers.) Each contestant tried to slide a pole toward a rolling hoop so that when the hoop toppled over it would rest on the end of the pole. The game was sacred, having been handed down before the people emerged into the upper world. The hoop and poles were prepared with elaborate ceremonies. Only men could play; women weren't allowed near the playing space.

We hadn't been too long in St. Augustine when the Army sent soldiers to round up all the Apache children. Children from the ages of eight to twenty years were taken forcibly from their parents. The parents resisted by holding onto their children as tightly as they could. Sometimes it took several soldiers to wrench one child from a mother who clung to the child with all her strength.

Of all the outrages we had to endure, this was the worst, Tsis-tohn said. Our women hid the children by putting them under the dresses of the older women. The soldiers weren't interested in older women; they liked to harass the younger women and those with children.

It was the same old story. The White Eyes were not going to permit us to stay together as families. We were too strong that way. We could endure anything, as long as we stayed together.

A boy named Johnny Loco was one of the Apache children who was able to escape by hiding under the skirts of his grandmother's dress.

Chief Chihuahua was given the choice as to which one of his children he could keep with him. He chose Eugene Chihuahua, who became my best friend. The rest were taken a long way off to the Carlisle Boarding School in Pennsylvania's Cumberland Valley. Those children who were nursing (like me) or not able to walk stayed at Fort Marion.

The Army sent the children to the school because they felt it was important that they learn how to live like white people. They needed to learn English. They needed to wear the White Eyes' clothing. They did not ask the parents for their okay. They did not explain what they were doing or why. They simply took the children away.

It was then that many parents gave up hope of ever returning to the Chiricahua Mountains. Many of the men and women simply lay down and died of a broken heart. The White Eyes did not think we had any feelings; they believed they could do whatever they wanted with our children. They did not know that we were a spiritual people who believed in a Creator and a Supreme Being; they considered us savages, incapable of those kinds of feelings.

Morning and nights in the confines of the dungeon of San Marcos, we prayed to our Creator to help us get our children back. Apaches are very close to their children; they love them deeply. The parents were convinced that the Army intended to kill the children and then kill the rest of us. We cried each night for the safety of our children. We prayed that they might be returned to our custody where they belonged.

The soldiers yelled at us when we spoke the Apache language. So did the scouts, whom the Army had betrayed into thinking they would be treated differently. They weren't. They were treated like the rest of us — as prisoners of war. We never forgave the scouts for what they did to us during those terrible days. Bad blood lingers to this day. It was a terrible time.

It was when the children were taken forcibly from us that we began to die from starvation, the damp rooms, the crowded conditions, hot weather, insects, and bad food. We were issued food that we had never eaten before; many of us refused to eat or even cook the food that we were given. The beef was okay, the potatoes, the flour we used to bake our daily bread; the rest we tossed to the birds.

The Army didn't feed us enough. They had the food but they wouldn't give it to us. We believe it was a deliberate effort on their part to starve us. The one thing that all of us remember about the Florida experience was that we were always hungry.

We suffered miserably behind the damp walls of the old fortress; at night, we were forced to sleep on the cold floors with only a straw pallet to cushion us. In the early morning, we sat in the first beams of sunlight as they warmed our bodies to a comfortable temperature. We didn't have enough clothes. Sometimes the only clothes we had were what we had brought with us from Arizona. There weren't nearly enough blankets or coats.

When the next trainload of Chiricahua arrived from Arizona, there was hardly any place in the fort where they could bed down. As a result, we lived packed on top of each other like bricks. The Army put up tents for us to sleep in on the bastions and the walkways and the terreplein. By this time there were hundreds of us living as best we could in every open spot of the fortress. We had two toilets, one for the men, another for the women, located close to the spot where we drew our water.

The weather was hot, the air sticky. At times, it became unbearably hot, even in the shade. We never could escape the heat. People complained of being dizzy from the coughing sickness (tuberculosis); they complained of a pain in their heads and eyes. One by one we began to die in the terrible Florida climate. We couldn't adjust to it. We came from the cool, high mountains of Arizona, where the air was healthy and fresh; that first year twenty-three children died.

My mother Tah-Tzil-Toey told me that I was born sometime in the year of 1886 in the old Spanish fort of Castillo de San Marcos in St. Augustine, Florida. She remembered that I came into the world on a hot day. I don't know if I was an easy birth or not. Tah-Tzil-Toey was separated from her husband Fun when he was sent to Fort Pickens in Pensacola with Nana and Chief Naiche and Geronimo. She said she was very pregnant during the long train ride from Arizona to Florida, and that it was a miracle she didn't miscarry.

C O N G E R

Established in 1565 by Don Pedro Menéndez de Avilés, St. Augustine is the oldest permanent European settlement in the continental United States. Begun in 1672 but not completed until 1695, the *castillo* replaced nine successive wooden fortifications that had protected St. Augustine from enemies since its founding. The castillo's baptism of fire came in 1702 during the War of the Spanish Succession, when the English occupied St. Augustine and laid siege (unsuccessfully) to the fort for fifty days. Before they departed, the English burned the town, but the castillo emerged unscathed, followed by another century of back-and-forth warfare by the European powers and their native allies.

Spain needed Florida as a refuge from which to guard the vital sea routes between Mexico and Europe. Creaky galleons, packed with bars of gold and silver, plied the waters between the continents. French and English corsairs, lurking in the bays and inlets on both sides of the Florida peninsula, raided the Spanish fleets as they plowed east to the port of Cádiz with their loads of precious metal.

The Chiricahua Apache were not the first American natives to be incarcerated in the old fort. Seminole Indians from two earlier wars, fighting against the U.S. Army in the 1830s and 1840s in the Florida Everglades, spent time there before being transferred to Fort Moultrie in South Carolina. Their leader, Osceola, was tricked into surrendering to the U.S. Army, just as Mangas Coloradas had been in Arizona in 1863. His decapitated head was boiled in an iron pot 'til the flesh and hair melted away; the skull was later exhibited in sideshows all over the country.

By 1875, the castillo had returned to its role as a place of imprisonment for Native Americans. The newest inmates came from the Great Plains and included Cheyenne, Arapaho, Comanche, and Kiowa people. Captain Richard Pratt was their warden, a progressive, humane officer; under his enlightened direction, the prisoners not only learned to read and speak English, they were allowed to sell hand-made trinkets to tourists. They also entertained guests at local hotels by performing authentic dances and demonstrating their archery skills.

WATSON

The white women from the St. Joseph Catholic Church in St. Augustine brought clothes, shoes, and hats for our people. They brought blankets when the nights were cold. These women insisted on being called "sister," even though they were not our relatives. It was explained to us that they were called "sisters" because they belonged to the Catholic Church.

I was baptized at the fort by the sisters and given a letter stating that I had been "christened." As if to counteract the influence of these gentle ladies, my mother told me the creation story of the Apache people. She told me about the Mountain Spirits in Arizona. She told me that the name of our creator was "Ussen."

Life at Fort Marion was full of peril. When new families arrived, the ones already there had to make room for them. The crowded conditions accelerated the pace at which contagious diseases such as small pox, pneumonia, malaria, and tuberculosis spread among the prisoners. Sanitary facilities were limited. There were only two latrines for some 500 people, and these were located near the wells where the prisoners obtained their drinking water.

The Army estimated that maximum occupancy of the entire fort should not exceed more than 150 people. The medical staff consisted of two orderlies, who did what they could to alleviate the suffering. The inmates continued to die. Corpses were carried in boats to nearby Anastasia Island, where they were buried in the sand dunes on the ocean side or tossed overboard, in flagrant violation of Apache taboos. To compound the outrage, the bones of the deceased frequently washed up on shore.

CONGER

With each new trip to Lawton, Oklahoma, I get to know Harry better. He's an engaging guy, humorous, with a deeply serious side. He tells me stories about the Chiricahua. In the 1890s and early 1900s they were driven by historical circumstances to the brink of extinction. Primarily because of their collective deep and enduring spirituality, they managed to survive. There are so many aspects to their lives that I don't see or know about. In addition to dealing with the same mundane matters as the rest of us — family, taxes, mortgages — they have access to an entirely different range of experience. They coexist in a kind of parallel universe that's steeped in the spirit and symbols of their native mythology. There's no lumping them together in a faceless mass; they are their own people, tough and resilient.

On one of my early trips to Lawton I met Harry's brother, Melvin. Melvin is Watson Mithlo's youngest child. According to Harry, Melvin is a medicine man. I believe it. There's something otherworldly about him. He knows all the secrets, all the stories. I'm wary of him at the same time I'm attracted to the bold and darkly serious attitude he radiates. He is Indian to the bone.

I find myself full of curiosity and affection for the Chiricahua. I want to learn as much as I can about them. At the same time there are limits to what they can tell me. At first this paradox puzzled me: How can I write with any authority about them if they don't tell me what I want to know?

It's more complicated than that. As an old Comanche woman who lived way out on the prairie once told me, "You took everything we had." In response to my request to hear a traditional story she retorted, "Why should we give you our stories? They are all that we have left."

Eugene slips out of the tipi to run an errand for Lavera, toiling in the cook shack with the other women. But Harry still has a devoted following, namely myself, rolled up in the buffalo robe against the growing afternoon chill. I sense that he's not finished yet and has more to say. Sure enough, after Eugene disappears Harry settles into a canvas-backed chair and clasps his fingers in a loose knot, bending his thumbs like fishhooks. The palm of his left hand pulses with a fleshy red glow. Now what's that all about? I wonder.

Harry tells me stories about UFOs. That gets my attention quick. He knows how to yank the white boy's chain, but I don't care. I'm a sucker for a good story, no matter how far-fetched it may be.

In April 2008, in the van on the way to Florida, he told a doozy to Andy Wilkinson and me. Andy, a series editor at Texas Tech University Press, was driving the van in which we were riding from Lawton, Oklahoma, to St. Augustine, Florida, where Harry intended to conduct a ceremony for those Apaches who died while languishing in the San Marco dungeons. It was the fuzzy-ball story I had heard before. One evening, on the outskirts of Lawton, a fuzzy, incandescent, ball-shaped object had pursued Harry's car. No matter how fast he drove, the object stayed with him. It finally jumped from his car to another coming from the opposite direction and disappeared.

Harry (smooth, deadpan manner, from the depths of the backseat of the van.): "It's happened to me more than once. I can't explain it."

He examined his fingertips. He could be maddeningly nonchalant when he wanted to be. "They seem to want me for something."

Andy was silent. So was I. Harry shrugged. "You should've seen the way that thing bounced and glistened. Like a basketball throwing off bright silver sparks."

He paused and looked directly at me. "You ought to write a book about UFOs in Indian territory."

I nearly swallowed my tongue.

"Only trouble is," he added, "there's a lot of stuff you don't know, and lots of stuff I can't tell you."

He chuckled. A puckish grin lit up his plump cheeks. He took advantage of the lull to launch into another story.

"It's a story I like to tell," he declared. "I call it 'The Little People's Gift: The Paint Horse.'"

He smiles broadly. He's in his element, now.

HARRY

A long time ago, when animals could talk, there was a young warrior who had a herd of horses. He raised their colts and trained the horses to be used in time of war. The young man had many tall horses, fast horses, quick horses, long-distance horses, and high-spirited horses. The horses were black, white, red, tan, gray, and orange. He was pleased with all of his horses but he longed for a very special one — one that was unique.

He decided he would ride out onto the prairie and ask the spirit for a horse — one that he would be proud of and one that would stand out among all the other horses. The warrior would search the prairies and hills for a new horse — a special one to bring back to the herd. One bright morning, he rode out in the direction of the big hill where the sun sits.

He found a small rise where he could sit and watch for his special horse. He prayed and waited for the spirit to hear his plea. Before long it was nighttime, and the warrior became sleepy and fell into a deep slumber.

The next morning, he awakened to the sound of knocking under his blanket. He lay very still, listening keenly. Again, he heard the knocking. Something was pressing against his back. When he heard a scratching sound under his blanket, he jumped up and pulled the blanket to the side. A small lid of earth rose up and a tiny person climbed out and spoke.

"'You went to sleep upon the entrance of our door and we couldn't get out."

The little man demanded, "Why are you so far from your people?"

The warrior stood entranced, as more Little People came out of the hole in the ground. They sat around him in a half-moon. They looked at him. He looked at them.

The warrior finally said, "I have many horses but I asked the spirit to give me a special horse — a different one from all the other horses."

The little man replied, "All right. Fair enough. In the morning you will have a special one."

The warrior moved his blanket off to the side and away from the Little People's entrance. The little man asked the others to go out and gather the colors from the earth and bring them back. "I will mix them for the warrior's horse."

The warrior watched and waited and tried his best to stay awake. The air was growing dark. Soon, he became so sleepy that once again he fell into a deep slumber.

The next morning, when the warrior opened his eyes, he remembered the vivid dream about the Little People. He looked around. There were no Little People. His horse was tied to a nearby mesquite tree, standing proudly, pawing at the ground. His tail had been tied up into a magnificent braid. He was painted in many different earth colors. There were patterns and shapes in these colors and they were all very unusual. This horse was different from any horse the warrior had ever seen. The warrior gave thanks to the spirit and to the Little People for the special gift of his paint horse.

CONGER

Something I noticed about Harry on the long drive from Lawton to St. Augustine is that he can see stuff all the way around in a circle. In the van driving all those hours he's quick to pick up grass fires in the distance, columns of yellow-gray smoke twirling along the pallid wastes of the panhandle horizon, strange cloud formations, curious birds. Moments like this, he has a kind of circumfluent vision, even while sitting enclosed in the back seat of a van with a Texas Tech logo on the front door. I think he can see around corners and behind walls and on the other side of hills and trees, with a kind of uncanny retinal elasticity. Geronimo supposedly had this capacity. "Second sight," I think it's called.

When Harry was in the Navy serving on a destroyer, the captain wanted him up on the bridge as often as possible, because he could spot things even before they were picked up on radar.

Indians are supposed to be able to tap into this stuff. (Some Indians, not all.) Extrasensory perception. Melvin is the shaman, he ought to know, although maybe Harry knows too. Harry's been urging me to go ahead and discuss any subject I want to with Melvin, including health issues, but so far I haven't been able to muster the nerve. It's hard for me, in conversation, to be direct and to the point.

Midway through the oration, I usually become acutely self-conscious. It's hard for me to importune someone, especially in regard to such an intensely private matter. My excuse today is that I need more time. I need to get to know the Mithlo brothers better.

Apache mystery seems to hover near the surface of things, which makes them more accessible — or maybe this was once the case, but no more. Too many objects have gotten in the way: automobiles, buildings, windmills, electronic devices. Four years ago, up on the Brulé (Lakota) reservation in South Dakota, an elder named Albert White Hat told me that when he was a boy the medicine men used to duel with each other in broad daylight, standing a few yards apart like old-time gunslingers, firing off one amazing trick after another. Coaxing rain clouds, for example, to dump their loads on a crowd of Miniconjou people standing across the way. Bam! One shaman would release a crow from his sleeve and the other would counteract by flooding the ground with gibbering mice. "But," said Albert, "there are fewer and fewer places where this kind of energy can be exercised. Today, there are too many electronic devices to make it work. Too many airplanes and automobiles, too many wires and cables. Oh, it's still out there and available, but it's more difficult to find. It's getting more difficult to locate the plugs. Now, we have to do it at night, in some forgotten corner of the reservation."

Albert's genial face darkened as if cast in a deep shadow. "The ground the shamans stood on once was sacred, and sacred land is getting harder to find. If we could just leave it alone for a few centuries, it would come back. I'm confident of it." The land really knows how to rebound. Look at what happened to the glaciers when they melted. But we continue to drill and dig and destroy. We have reduced an entire cosmos to a patchwork quilt bedecked with tattered scraps and tags, all in the name of "civilizing" the landscape and purging the "Indianness" from it.

And then something happened that was to change everything.

One day when I was in Lawton, I told Harry that I intended to go to Chiricahua National Monument in southeast Arizona to see for myself what the Apache homeland was like. Harry's face lit up with a smile.

"There's no reason why I can't do this, is there?" I asked.

"Heck, no," Harry replied. "It's a wild, free world down there, and you can go anywhere you like."

I brooded on this awhile. It was symptomatic of me in any new adventure first to find out what the parameters were — the limits, the distances between the nodal points, the boundaries. Before embarking on any new adventure, I first had to know what the outside limits were and how long it would take me to cover that ground. (What can I do, and when can I do it?) A product of my upbringing, I suppose; it seems as if my orderly, middle-class mind functions best within the hash marks of a measurable span.

Harry told me that when I got to the top of Sugarloaf Mountain I should find a flat rock and sit down. "Just you sit there awhile and listen," he said, pointing a chunky digit at my chest. "You'll be surprised. You won't know what it is at first, and then you'll recognize it. You'll hear the sound of an old-time Apache encampment. People, children, horses, dogs, fires, smoke, wind. The way they used to live back in the old days."

I flew to Tucson from Kansas City, rented a car, and drove to Chiricahua National Monument. It was mid-afternoon when I got up to the top of Sugarloaf Mountain and sat down as Harry had told me to do. Fortunately, there were few people. (Being alone is a necessary condition for experiencing any kind of extrasensory feeling or insight.) The crown of this mountain complex is a jagged maze of spires and columns — totems, hoodoos, balanced rocks — carved out of the soft, friable tuff that constitutes the majority of the material of which these mountains are made. Around thirty million years ago, fiery volcanic clouds rumbled down the slopes and spread out over the surrounding region, while other clouds rose high into the sky in billowing black clots, sleeting a fine, particulate matter as they expanded and cooled.

I strolled along a trail that slanted in a southerly direction around the rim of a broad basin packed with towering pines. There was something mesmeric in the steady back-and-forth motion of the wind against the pliable tips. This went on for a while. I didn't hear any voices or other camp sounds, just the creak of the wind, blowing in from the south, all the way from Mexico. Then suddenly the pine tips began to pop and bubble like fermented balls of color, green and gold primarily, tiny and intense, noiselessly crackling in a well of perfect silence, a cool, deep, arboreal immensity against which the tiny balls flared like strings of incandescent beads.

I was dumbfounded. "What's that all about?" I muttered to myself.

The whole thing lasted maybe five minutes. It's hard to delineate. I was too dazed and elated to regard the scene objectively. The balls of color danced and shivered, popping straight up in the air or tumbling laterally across the top of the basin, flickering like pool balls across the green baize of a table.

I sat down and clasped my fingers together. My hands trembled. I have Parkinson's, but it was more than that. It was a phenomenon, a bona fide event, bizarre and otherworldly.

A few days later, when I finally got up the nerve to tell Harry what I had seen, he was delighted. "Well, you seen 'em, all right."

"Seen what?"

"The mountain spirits. They're all over the place up there. And you seen 'em, okay. There's Apache full-bloods older than you who go up there and they haven't ever seen a hint of them."

He looked at me with an affectionate grin. "You are one weird white boy," he said.

This was the first of the events that were to bring me close to something I didn't really understand, and didn't really know if I ever would. I don't mean to sound cavalier; I was thrilled to the marrow of my bones to have witnessed those little balls of concentrated energy popping liquidly before my eyes at the top of Sugarloaf Mountain in the heart of the Chiricahuas. At the same time I was skeptical; what right did I, a non-Native person, have to observe such a phenomenon? On the other hand, maybe it was an illusion, projected from the depths of my imagination, a dazzling display of exotic information, kinked and knotted with arcane data, twisty and odd.

Something was going on, but I didn't know what.

WATSON

As soon as we got to Fort Marion, Chief Chihuahua and others began to lobby the Army strenuously for us to serve out our sentence in a more congenial location. Despite our abject condition, we weren't without some influential friends. Herbert Welsh of the powerful Indian Rights Association in Philadelphia visited Fort Marion in March of 1887 and wrote a scathing account of the conditions there. Six months after we first entered the dungeon, the government still had not provided any new clothing. Many prisoners were still sleeping without blankets on cold bricks; food rations had not improved, leading Welsh to conclude that "the intent of the American government toward the Chiricahua Apache was to starve them."

The report caused an uproar in the American press.

Welsh blasted the fort's sanitary conditions. "The danger of contagious disease attacking these Indians is, in my judgement, a matter worthy of prompt and serious consideration."

Welsh concluded his report with a blistering critique of the plight of the Chiricahua scouts, who were imprisoned in Fort Pickens alongside the Apache warriors they had helped capture or convince to surrender.

CONGER

A dramatic indication of the resilience of the Chiricahua Apache was the appearance before them of the Mountain Spirits while they were imprisoned at Fort Marion. I don't know the process by which a decision of this magnitude is reached by the people in charge, but I was told by Melvin Mithlo that the very existence of the tribe must be threatened by circumstances seemingly beyond their control. By February 1887, the condition of the Chiricahua was dire; twenty-three children had died and many more had fallen ill. They were in real danger of losing more people than they could replace. Fearful of extinction, they appealed to the Spirits. Led by a shaman named Zah-mon, the dancers improvised their own musical instruments, using whatever natural materials they could find. Zah-mon had left his drum in Arizona, so he devised a new one, drawing a soapy rag tightly over the mouth of an iron kettle. The drumstick was fashioned from a willow branch, with a loop at one end. While the medicinal plants from the Southwest were missing, the dancers had brought their sacred paint with them. Each dancer wore a different yellow design on his back and chest. Zigzag snakes and lightning bolts decorated their arms. Arizona was a long way from Fort Marion, but the dance in all its shimmering intensity brought the two locations closer together.

How did the Chiricahua manage to arrange this event? Was it held clandestinely in a discreet corner of the fortress? Who persuaded the authorities that it was a good idea? I suspect the influence of Herbert Welsh was critical. The last thing the Army needed concerning the Apache was more bad publicity. The mood in America was changing; from being viewed as bloodthirsty savages, Indians were slowly being transformed in image and memory to a benign icon, devoid of threat or danger.

As Zah-mon thumped his drum, the dancers finished daubing their bodies with sacred colors. An ailing child lying in a tent with his mother close by was the object of their solicitations. Inside the tent, the dancers bobbed and ducked, stabbing the air with their staves and stomping their feet to drive the evil spirits away.

Presently, the woman came out of the tent, holding her sick baby up to the dancers. The spirits swooshed their holy sticks around, over and under the cradleboard. Each of the dancers then took the child in his hands, pressed it to his breast, raised the cradleboard to the sky, then lowered it to a cacophony of shrieks, yells, and ululations from the mother and the other women.

HARRY

"The origin of the Dance of the Mountain Spirits goes back a long way in Apache culture and history," Harry said to me one day as we sat on the bank of Medicine Creek in the heart of the Fort Sill compound. "Gah'e, as these spirits are called, tell a really old story." The sky was filled with smooth, early summer clouds. A sweet breeze laced with the scent of fresh grass lapped our faces.

Two young Apache men were physically disabled—one blind, the other lame. Because they could not travel fast enough during an enemy attack, they were left to fend for themselves.

The families chose a cave in a remote hillside where the two men could hide with enough provisions to enable them to survive until the tribe came back to get them. As they huddled together deep in the cave, curious figures wearing elaborate headdresses crept out of the darkness. Among these figures was an agile creature wearing buckskin but no headdress; his body was painted white, and he seemed to possess greater power and stamina than his companions. This was the Mountain Spirit, who spoke to the two men in a kindly tone. "Do not be frightened. Have courage. We come as gods from the four directions. We come to relieve you of your suffering and deliver you to the safety of your people."

The agile white figure motioned to his companions, and instantly an eerie chant warbled through the cave. A ball of fire dropped at their feet, and the spirits began to dance around this fire.

There looked to be no set pattern to the dance. Each spirit stamped and postured on his own. The wind howled from the four directions, accompanied by a pelting rain. The white-painted spirit gestured and stomped. At intervals, a soft keening could be heard. The two men—one blind, the other crippled—believed that a woman, the mother of the power that created all life on earth, was making this sound. The Mountain Spirits continued to wave their staffs.

At the end of the dance, the two men were guided by the gods through the cave entrance and along a trail, toward a big rock that hung over the entrance. The white-painted god led the way; he ran up to the rock and struck it with his staff. The rock flew open, revealing a narrow passageway.

As the blind man passed through, he regained his sight, while the lame man's legs were restored. The two men were clothed in the finest buckskin attire and beautifully ornamented boots. Each carried a carved bow and a clutch of gleaming arrows.

In the distance, they saw an Apache encampment, and they set out to rejoin their people. The people did not immediately recognize them, but only after they had described the mystic deeds they had witnessed in the cave. So moved were the Apaches by the story they wanted to see the mountain spirits for themselves. They jumped on their horses, but were unable to move; the horses had turned to stone.

Some Apaches believe the Dance of the Mountain Spirits commemorates the onset of maidenhood in a pubescent girl. Others believe the primary purpose of the dance is to maintain the strength and well-being of the people.

CONGER

Harry gazed at the gray-green surface of the sluggish stream that purled along the foot of Medicine Creek inside the Fort Sill military compound. Was he seeing something he hadn't seen before? The stream's steady, serpentine crawl across the rumpled face of the broken prairie suggested more than just a conventional watering source. There were things in there that Harry could see, and that I couldn't. Apaches were wary of water. Harry remembered once being pelted by pebbles from the brook spat out by an impish spirit. He was a teenager, he'd come down to the creek with his buddies to smoke and talk. As soon as they sat down, the spirit bombarded them with pebbles. Harry remembered how they had run away from the stream as fast as their legs could carry them. He chuckled. Watson had told him to be careful of water.

The thought staggered me. How could one person be susceptible to this phenomenon and not other people? Was it a matter of possessing certain DNA that stirred and stoked the plethora of visions he experienced every day? Behind this reality there were others, how many was impossible to say, layer upon layer, stacked like transparent panels in a mounded hump that reached all the way to the moon. I was bewildered.

Was Harry pulling a fast one to catch the attention of the gullible white boy? Fish spitting was not a feature of my culture.

Harry, Andy, and I arrive at St. Augustine on March 18, 2009, at 10:30 p.m. after an exhausting fourteen-hour drive from Natchitoches, Louisiana. Andy drove the entire way. We settle in a Best Western motel across the street from the Castillo de San Marcos.

Nine o'clock the next morning we're met at the entrance by National Park Service ranger Amy Harper, a comely woman with chestnut eyes and long hair pulled back into a smooth ponytail. She escorts us across the bridge spanning the dry moat into the fortress. Harry detaches himself from our company before we reach the end of the bridge; at breakfast, he indicated he would need to drift about on his own. "The feel of the spirits was strong everywhere I went in San Marco," he said later. "I could feel them pressing against me. They seemed disturbed by my presence. I don't think they knew what was happening."

I stick close to Harry. Andy and Amy proceed without us. The previous week, I had asked Amy over the phone if we could ramble around the fortress, that we were a party of people from Lawton, Oklahoma, providing escort for an Apache elder whose father had been born in captivity on the premises in 1886. Amy was delighted to grant our every wish.

I have my own tenuous attachment to the castillo, dating back to 1950 when I was nine years old and drove here from Kansas City with my brother and parents on vacation. The memory is sketchy, a montage of recognizable images, arrayed across the canvas of my past like stick figures on a blank wall. What's it like to be in the presence of one's ancestors on a historical site where these spirits, in full flesh, once suffered egregiously and died? There ought to be some kind of linkage for all of us, a connection to the unknown and the ineffable. Maybe at one time there was, before our capacity for extrasensory awareness became clogged and cluttered by all the steel and plastic and electronic jabber that pollute our senses today.

Harry tells me that he will need me to help him work a few chores related to the ceremony he is about to perform. He wanders about, peering into casemates, strolling across bastions, looking, touching, holding his head still, listening. As far as he knows, he is the first Chiricahua Apache to make this pilgrimage to San Marco. Amy and

Andy inspect the guard rooms, the ravelin, the powder magazine. Midmorning, a sizable crowd mills about the monument, vacationers from New England and the Atlantic coast, judging by their dress and accents.

Harry points in the direction of the Plaza de Armas, where, out of the wind, next to an embrasure, we secure the deer-hide tympanum to the bowl-shaped drum with taut rubber bands. The hide is pulpy and white, resistant to our tugs and pulls; the bands stretch to the snapping point as we work them around and over the rim of the bowl. Harry takes a curved stick from his pocket and taps it against the skin. Since he is not hearing the resonance he wants, we add two more bands, clamping the skin tighter to the bowl-shaped frame, fingers taut and strained, feeling the skin stretch to the breaking point. Harry taps the surface again and seems pleased with what he hears.

He steps across a grassy sward at the center of the plaza, to a circular spot several feet in diameter. He kneels down on the spot and runs his thumb through the dry grass; then he takes out a white pouch primed with hoddentin (cattail pollen), a dark, glistening, reddish-yellow powder, and scatters a pinch or two inside the circle of mixed green and brown grass. A light wind lifts a delicate skein of pollen across the grass, salting the sleeve of my shirt, my cheeks, and my neck, before whirling out of view.

Harry rises slowly to his feet. Tapping the drum with the stick, he commences to sing, gazing up at the soft blue sky, his deep, resonant voice clearly audible over the sound of the wind fluttering through the plaza. People wandering the plaza or climbing the ramps or standing on the terreplein at the top of the fortress hear the voice and drum and slow to a stop, looking around. Who is this huge, honey-bear of an Indian man standing in the center of the courtyard, singing in an ancient language? Harry sings some more, the sounds rolling off his palate with a rhythmic lilt. He then beckons and I pass him a hand-rolled cigarette. He singes the tip, puffs meditatively, hands it back to me. I puff and pass it to Andy. The smoke curls into the sky. The visitors, eyes wide, look on in astonishment.

Harry told me later, "As I sang I could feel the spirits of the ancestors leave the fortress. That was why we were there: to release the spirits, to let them go free. I told them the time was now. They had been here long enough."

For another hour we wander around the fortress, poking into rooms, asking questions, with Amy Harper helpfully explaining this and that.

There's no reason I should find myself in the middle of this. Culturally, my upbringing was conventional: WASP, Midwestern, middle class. I came from a family of amiable drunks, boisterous, fun-loving people, who liked to laugh and pass the laughter on. As a kid I had a predictably stereotyped attitude toward Indians.

My good pal George Olendorf and I one afternoon early in our lives (we must have been seven or eight) were besieged in the backyard of his red brick house by a band of whooping Indians who circled our covered wagon on their sweaty ponies. It invariably happened this way once a week after school and maybe twice on Saturday, especially after watching a western B movie downtown at the Orpheum or the Missouri theaters staring Joel McCrea or Randolph Scott, two of our favorites, along with Victor Jory, a cruel sneer mapping his dark, scowling face, cast as Geronimo or Cochise or Victorio.

How much fun it was to blast away with our imaginary guns and pot them one by one, watching them fall off their ponies and sprawl in the desert sand while their fellow warriors continued to circle the wagon, which by this time had caught fire from a barrage of flaming arrows. George and I took turns getting plugged by an arrow fired by a dusky warrior, grappling with the shaft, falling backwards off the stone ledge of the outdoor oven, kicking and writhing. A bunch of silly make-believe, until the game turned serious and we began knocking off the headmen one by one. First the chief, bedecked in a full bonnet of eagle feathers, who went down easily under George's keen aim, leaving no one important for me to knock off. "You get the medicine man!" George shouted over the slush of gunfire from the saliva sloshing between his puffy cheeks.

"Who's that?"

"Their religious leader!"

"A preacher?" I was thinking of the anemic, white-cheeked pastor who officiated on Sunday mornings in the local Methodist church my family attended.

"No, no!" George cried. He was far more knowledgeable about these matters than I. "He's the guy who has the magic. He can make the sun swallow the sky if he wants to."

So it went in White America in the bucolic Midwest in the late 1940s. Occasionally I got to knock off the chief and George took care of the medicine man. "That man," he said, as we took a break from our activity, "gets his power from the animal furs and feathers and bones he wears all over his body."

How George knew this, I don't know. He did go to the library a lot.

The only feathers I knew anything about were blue jay feathers, which I found in our yard. Held up to the sun, they glowed brilliantly. One time I came to the dinner table with several stuck in my hair. My brother scoffed; my mother looked out the window; my father told me to take them out. I did as I was told, knowing there were plenty more where they came from.

There's a photograph somewhere of my family in church, the Francis Street Methodist Church, which we attended regularly during my formative years, or at least as long as my grandmother was alive. A plump dumpling of a German woman, with a ready smile and an infectious laugh, she died in 1964 at the age of 86.

We were sitting stiffly in a church pew. I have no explanation for it. The pew was selected more likely by my grandmother as the spot we should occupy while someone (I have no idea who) snapped an impromptu family portrait.

There are five people in the photo: Mother, Dad, Bill (my older brother), myself, and grandmother Lena Bloom Albrecht (my mother's mother, whom we called "Gommie"). There's not a lot of pizazz in the photo. It's easy to trace the bloodlines that mark the members of my family, especially on the German side, from Gommie on down to my brother—the nose, the full lips, the large expressive eyes (especially the eyes!). I favor my father's side—French and English (who not typically known for being swarthy)—but which gives our skin, especially his, a distinct swarthy cast. Nobody seems very happy in the photo, although Gommie does manage to flash her radiant smile. The rest of us look worn-out and weary.

My mother did not like to be photographed under any circumstances, and she shows her displeasure by putting on her motherly mien and composing her attractive features into a bland, stolid mask. My father with his rakish good looks liked very much having his picture taken. (He had those finely chiseled features that made him look good from any angle.) Bill, my older brother (by four years), looks hostile and surly, charged with a load of pent-up anger that was to plague him all his life. And then there is me, a skinny little kid in my early teens, starting to puff around the jowls with the onset of puberty, although still (for the moment) apple-cheeked.

I suppose we were a happy family in that cushy, insulated 1950s kind of way. Dad owned a prosperous laundry and dry-cleaning establishment. We had plenty to eat and drink, a 21-inch Motorola TV in the living room, a new car in the garage — a Buick, mind you, not a Ford. Nonetheless, my mother's eyes remained wide and full of woe; my brother habitually curled his upper lip into a fiendish leer. I was well into my teens when I finally determined that basically we were an unhappy family, not dysfunctional but, apart from all the fun hijinks, there were deep flaws in the family unit. My brother wrecked every automobile he ever owned. Mother drank too much. Dad did too. I must have sensed something ominous about the future, so I decided to duck it by going to boarding school in Connecticut. I know I wanted my life to be radically different. What that would turn out to be, I had no way of knowing. A writer, perhaps, whatever that was. Or an Indian.

Two weeks after my father, Conger Sr., died at the age of 89 in 1997, I received a call from a former editor of the *St. Joseph News Press*. The man's name was Bob Slater, and he had worked for the paper for nearly fifty years in every capacity: reporter, editor, publisher.

There was a distinct pause after he tendered his formal regrets. Bob Slater used to play gin rummy with my father during the lunch hour at the Benton Club, in downtown St. Jo. "Tony," he said (Tony is my nickname), "don't get me wrong, but I always thought your dad was an Indian. His skin, hair, eyes, even the way he walked."

Other people had told me the same thing. My mother assumed he was part Italian. Suppose he was. What did it matter? Did my mother even care? Her people were German, originally from Munich. Stolid, big-limbed, fair-complexioned, people, with a healthy appetite for food and drink. The swarthy tone of Conger's skin I attributed to French blood from his mother's side. (She was a Conger — originally "Congier.")

The first real Indian I ever met was a guest speaker at a summer camp in Minnesota when I was twelve years old. I forget his name, but he was a Mandan from North Dakota. I didn't know anything about the Mandans then, but I never forgot this fellow; he carried himself with a certain air of distinction, a certain posture. No doubt he'd been asked to talk to the boys about his people, the Mandans, their history and culture. Probably he'd been invited to impart a different perspective to the wedding-cake whiteness of the majority of the campers who, ranging in age from six to eighteen, came from major cities in the Midwest.

He spoke English with an educated accent. Not that I expected anything different, but I knew he had his own language; our camp counselor had told us that morning that it was "a very ancient and beautiful language." The counselor was a college student from Oklahoma, so he had to know something about Indians.

The Mandan wasn't a big man, although his shoulders were solid and he looked muscular. Depending on the angle and intensity of the late-morning sun, he looked by turns calm and passive or imbued with the ferocity of a hawk. He wore a beaded buckskin jacket spangled with fetish-like objects and a pair of beaded moccasins; three golden-eagle feathers attached to his glossy, pitch-black hair dangled between his shoulder blades.

I hung around for a while with a couple of buddies, asking him questions. I remember that his hands were small, like my father's, delicate and fine-boned. His voice was a bit gruff, but that only added to his compelling image. He talked about the Mandans and how they were nearly exterminated by diseases brought upriver from St. Louis by white traders and trappers in the 1800s. It was the first time I had ever heard about that. When he smiled his prominent teeth glowed like a movie star's. The guy was definitely cool.

WATSON

About six months after we first came to Fort Marion, Chief Chihuahua announced that the White Eyes had agreed to let us move to the Mount Vernon Barracks in Alabama. We knew nothing about where that was; we had never heard of Alabama. We were told we would like it much better than Fort Marion. We could grow crops there and raise cattle and start a new life.

Our reaction to the Mount Vernon Barracks move was positive. We felt a renewed sense of hope. No more crowded cells, dreary dungeons, dismal conditions, or fatal diseases. Instead of tents, we would live in regular houses. Best of all, our children would not be taken from us and sent up north to schools that were little more than death traps.

It was a time of joy and sadness. A few of the children were allowed to come home to be with their families, and that was wonderful, although many of them had contracted the deadly coughing sickness, which the White Eyes call tuberculosis. Many, after coming back home, took sick and died. The disease was contagious; old men, women, and little children were especially susceptible.

The returning children told stories of the many ways in which they were abused at the school in Carlisle. They were taught that if they were asked a question, they were to respond with a "yes." Many did not understand what was being asked, but they said "yes" anyway. Sometimes they were asked questions that accused them of something and made them blush with shame. Such as "Who did this?" and "Who is responsible for this job not being done?" The students would be punished severely when they answered "yes." So they learned not to say anything.

They were also punished for speaking their native language with their fellow students. As a result, many students became frustrated and despondent. Apache families are very close. Many missed their parents and siblings so desperately they gave in to the illness and died.

Several families sponsored a special blessing dance that lasted four days to help heal the sick students. The families gave away all their belongings to help restore their youngsters' health. Each day, the medicine man treated the sick person with sacred pollen. The pollen was sprinkled on the feet, legs, body, and head.

The medicine men were honorable men, held in high esteem by our people. They maintained the rituals and traditions during this terrible time in our history. For the most part, they were decent and principled, with the well-being of the people foremost in their thoughts.

During the six years we were detained at the Mount Vernon Barracks, the prisoners attempted to resume their lives according to the customs they had followed when they were free. They gathered the children around the campfires and repeated over and over the people's history, myths, and traditional stories. They trained the dancers and performed the rites of the puberty ceremonials. They celebrated weddings according to ancient custom. The young boys played the hoop-and-pole game, given to them by the animals. The adolescent boys were required to make the four-day fast and prayer in order to receive the vision of the totem that would serve as their primary medicine for the rest of their lives. The young men were trained in the old-fashioned manner to become warriors, first serving as gofers to the older men, feeding them, taking care of their horses, replenishing their water casks, making sure their weapons were in perfect order.

The Mount Vernon Barracks was located on the west bank of the Mobile River, about thirty miles from the port town of Mobile, Alabama. The grounds were shrouded with deep shadows cast by pine and deciduous trees that blocked off the afternoon sun. If somebody wanted to view the sunset, he had to climb a forty-foot tree to find it. The grounds were much more spacious than those we had been afforded at Fort Marion, enabling us to move around and visit other families. In the old days, the Chiricahua lived in family clusters within calling distance of one another—far enough apart to give each settlement a sense of privacy yet close enough to help each other when necessary. At Mount Vernon, we were able for the first time in many years to practice the rituals that are a vital part of our culture: the dance of the Mountain Spirits, puberty and marriage ceremonies, young warrior rituals, girls coming of age. We danced into the night and enjoyed ourselves as a free people. We weren't free; we were prisoners of war and would remain so for seven more years—but after the cramped confines of the Castillo de San Marcos, it felt like freedom. The elders told us the stories they had heard as youngsters, how the Apache people came to be. This way, despite the hardships, despite living far away from our native land, despite ongoing abuse and repression, we kept the culture alive.

The old men continued to sing the traditional songs and dance the traditional dances. Apaches love to celebrate and enjoy life and the glory of the natural world. It was good to watch our people come alive again.

While we were in Alabama many of the young men enlisted in the U.S. Army—not as scouts but as regular recruits—where they were trained and disciplined. The recruits received a modest payment, which helped their families acquire extra food and clothing. Dressed in wool uniforms, carrying fake rifles carved out of wood, they marched alongside the Mobile River in close formation, presided over by white noncommissioned officers. On the weekends, crowds of tourists from as far away as Mobile and Pensacola came to see the Apaches, especially the Warrior Geronimo, who joined us at the Barracks in 1887, after spending a year at Fort Pickens in Pensacola. At times, the recruits camped along the river for as long as a week. It was good for them to look and act like warriors again. They were natural fighters. They were Apache.

It was in Alabama that my mother Tah-tzil-Toey and her husband Fun were reunited as husband and wife. Unfortunately, their happiness was short-lived. One day in March 1892, Fun got angry with his wife. He believed she was flirting with the soldiers, and he became insanely jealous. He fired a gun at her. Distraught, he ran into the woods, placed the gun barrel against his forehead, and tripped the trigger with his bare toe.

Had he lived after wounding her, the Army would have hanged him. No Apache warrior wants to go through the afterlife with his neck twisted, his tongue protruding between his lips, his eyes bulging from their sockets.

An Apache medicine man cured my mother of her wounds. They were severe, but she survived. Later, she said that she was determined to live because of my sister Maggie and me. It was a sad time, but we persevered and picked up the pieces and moved on. We were Apaches. We were used to hardship and suffering.

In Alabama, we lived in small, square, wood-frame houses with dirt floors and no windows. In 1891, we built sturdier, more comfortable houses, painted outside and finished within, set on sturdy foundations. We cooked outdoors and ate together out of a large bowl with our fingers. Not all families had enough to eat, but what we didn't need we shared with others and they shared with us. The Apache way.

Alabama was hot and humid, but it wasn't as bad as Florida. The bugs and flies caused a lot of trouble. Mosquito bites drove us wild. The children tore at the bites with their fingernails, which became infected. The bugs were especially bad at night. We built big fires that threw out clouds of smoke to keep them at bay.

Our new home was full of trees, tall trees with thick bark that blocked the flow of the wind. Sometimes we sat for hours in pools of sweat. We worked hard to remove the heavy growth of brush under the trees. We didn't like snakes, and when one slithered into the house or wiggled across the roof, we made a commotion. Sometimes the soldiers had to come and get them out.

CONGER

Harry Mithlo liked what he saw at Mount Vernon, where we stopped for an hour or two after leaving Fort Marion and Saint Augustine for the long drive back to Lawton, Oklahoma. The landscape was steep and hilly, shadowed by dark, gloomy trees. The Chiricahua Apache left Fort Marion on April 27, 1887, stopping first in Pensacola to pick up the warriors — Naiche, Geronimo, Fun, Nana, Chihuahua, Loco, Mangas Coloradas, Chatto — who had been imprisoned there for eight months. The Barracks, as they were known, was to be their new home.

The Barracks had undergone several incarnations during its fifty-year existence; it had been a fort, a military post, a hospital, a psychiatric center. Built as a military post in the 1830s, it was encircled by a formidable brick wall. Harry liked the fact that the Chiricahua were free to roam the grounds pretty much where they wanted, all the way to the little village at the foot of the ridge on top of which the Barracks was situated, so long as they were back on the premises by dark. Considering the severity of their confinement at Fort Marion, this was a welcome sign.

A playful smile creased Harry's warm, jowly face after touring the Barracks. "This is where they got back together," he said. "They started to have children again. They got back into their rituals and ceremonies."

His sense of humor bubbled. As we walked out into the parking lot to get into the van to resume the journey back to Lawton, he noticed a wisp of smoke coiling into the sky from a fire down in the village. "Hey, boys," he called to Andy and me. "Looky here. Those Apaches are trying to burn down the town."

WATSON

No matter how much better our situation was, we were still plagued by the same diseases. A report filed by Lieutenant Guy Howard on December 23, 1897 stated that "in regards to conditions in Mount Vernon the camp was as good as a prison camp can be, but it cannot be made into a home." The mortality rate was appalling: eighty-nine deaths so far in Fort Marion, Fort Pickens, and Mount Vernon, plus thirty at the Carlisle school in Pennsylvania, which amounted to nearly one-fourth of the total population in the three-and-a-half years since the first party of Chiricahuas arrived in Florida in the spring of 1886.

Although life was a little better, we still missed the mountains of Arizona, our true home. We wanted to return to a country where we could see the sun without having to climb a tree.

On the weekends, white people from towns as far away as Pensacola came to see how we lived. They were curious about the Apache people, especially our warriors and chiefs. The better-known warriors sold trinkets and photographs of themselves; if they could write, they autographed the objects. Women sold straw baskets that they wove out of the fibers of stiff, wiry plants.

Although it was better than Florida, we didn't like Alabama and wanted to move somewhere else. We wanted to be free of the sickness that followed us wherever we went. We wanted to work the land. We wanted to raise cattle. We never had enough to eat. By this time, several Apaches understood English, but no American (with the exception of George Wratten) understood the complexities of the Apache language. How could an outsider comprehend our leaders when they tried to explain what we wanted? How could any outsider understand the hardships we had to endure?

Our leaders met regularly with the White Eyes, talking and communicating as best they could. For once, we both agreed that it would be best if we could move out west somewhere. We knew that returning to Arizona was out of the question — the new white settlers there would not permit it — but the Army thought we could find a place to live in the Oklahoma Territory, where many other Indians lived, somewhere in the vicinity of Fort Sill, in the southwest portion of the territory. We were told that the climate there was dry like that of the Arizona high country.

Some of our people were ready to move west to Fort Sill. Others didn't want to leave Alabama and go to a place they knew nothing about. The White Eyes had lied to us so many times, we didn't trust anyone anymore. We had been told of all the wonderful changes that would take place in our lives if we were only patient, and then of course nothing happened. No wonder we were jittery. No wonder we didn't know what would happen if we moved to Fort Sill.

We lived together pretty much as an extended family, the seven years we spent in Alabama. There was considerable improvement in our lives, but we needed and deserved a lot more. Husbands and wives got together again; children were born. The Army told us that if we moved to Oklahoma, we would be allowed to take only our clothing, cooking gear, and a few personal items. No furniture, cows, horses, dogs, or chickens. We didn't have many of those things anyway. Eventually, a decision was arrived at, and in their usual paranoid, secretive way, the cavalry led us away from the Mount Vernon Barracks in the middle of the night. We were put aboard a train in Mobile, Alabama, and headed west to Fort Sill. This time the windows were open and the doors were unlocked. Guards with guns watched us closely, but we had lavatories that we could use. People in the little towns along the way continued to look in the windows for a glimpse of the wild Apaches. This was in October 1894. I was eight years old.

The twelve-car train arrived at the little community of Rush Springs, Oklahoma Territory, with a squeal of brakes and a cloud of steam as the wheels locked and the locomotive slid along the shiny rails to a complete stop. A few Indians stood on the platform, gazing impassively at the newcomers who carried with them very little in the way of personal gear or material goods. The arrivals were Chiricahua Apaches, a short, wiry people, who disembarked hesitantly from the passenger cars and looked around. Some wore store-bought shoes bound with laces, others handcrafted boots, still others the traditional Apache moccasin turned up at the toe to protect their feet from cactus thorns. A few White Eyes crowded into the little station in the middle of the empty prairie to watch the newcomers get off the cars. Some waved and saluted, others shouted. I didn't understand what they were saying, or why they were waving. Tah-Tzil-Toey told me to stay close to my sister Maggie. "The White Eyes might steal her and sell her to the Mexicans," she said.

The station was packed with people with brown skin like mine. There were also lots of white people, men dressed in dark suits, women in fancy hats and dresses, other women in camp dresses with calico bonnets and soiled aprons. Like cats, the white people had eyes of colors other than black: green, blue, hazel, brown. I had never seen so many white people before. Nor had I seen that many brown-skinned people. The men wore thick, worsted trousers, white shirts, jackets, broad-brimmed hats, and boots. They smoked incessantly or chewed dark plugs of Bull Durham tobacco bunched like walnuts in their cheeks. Most of the White Eyes, women and men, were fat. They must be rich, I thought, with lots of money, who can buy all the food they want. I wondered if someday I'd be rich and fat. Later on, I learned that not all fat people were rich, and not all rich people were fat.

A company of soldiers officered by Second Lieutenant Allyn Capron waited at the foot of the station platform to escort us to our new home at Fort Sill. Accompanying them was a contingent of Indian scouts on horseback and clad in military jackets; puffed up with their own self-importance, they wore thin, braided, blood-red lanyards dangling from their hair. A few of the Indian men waiting on the platform tried to talk to the Apaches, but they couldn't make themselves understood. The scouts tried to communicate with sign language, but the Apache men didn't know this system, or pretended not to. The Apaches spoke Spanish to the scouts, but the scouts said they couldn't understand Spanish, which wasn't true. Why was everyone behaving in such a contrary manner? I couldn't understand it then, and I can't understand it now. Each side finally had to produce a Carlisle boy from their ranks so they could make their needs known to each other in English.

It was a long trek, more than twenty miles, from the Rush Springs station to our new home. The sick, infirm, and decrepit rode in wagons; everyone else walked. Accompanying us were huge wagons with tall, creaky wheels, loaded with freight and supplies destined for Fort Sill and the outlying hamlets. The Rush Spring station dropped from view behind us as we proceeded steadily across the smooth, rolling prairie. We hadn't been in an open landscape like this for a long time. Flocks of birds filled the sky; the dry autumn grass smelled crisp and sweet. The feel of the wind was much more pleasant than what we had known in Alabama and Florida. The horses that the scouts and soldiers rode gave off a strong odor as they walked ahead of us. I watched their long legs, followed the bobbing rhythm of their heads, and listened to the clop of their unshod hooves. Someday I would own a horse so I could explore this new country that I had heard so much about but until now had never seen with my own eyes.

A feeling of excitement and expectation ran through us as the gray blade of a distant mountain rose up on the western horizon. These were the Wichita Mountains, an ancient range composed of piles of shattered rock, massive boulders, and weedy pastures named after the tribe that once roamed this region. The more we walked the more excited we became. Most of us had not seen a real mountain since we left Arizona in 1886. I had never seen a mountain. I was as excited as the old people. They spoke of the deer, turkey, javelina, and birds and how they tasted when roasted over a fire. They spoke about camping in shallow arroyos next to cliff faces beaded with bubbles of fresh spring water.

All day that first day in Oklahoma, we marched steadily toward Fort Sill, twenty miles to the west. We stopped that evening alongside a creek near the present-day town of Elgin. The women lit campfires; that night we huddled around them for warmth. Mother fashioned a shelter from the young trees by pulling the branches over to form a dome that she covered with blankets to keep out the cold.

That night the elders talked about the many different Indians — Comanche, Kiowa, Kiowa Apache, Wichita, and Caddo — who lived on the land around Fort Sill. This land was new and strange to the Apache. We had no idea how long we were going to live there. The Army had told us that this was to be our new home; for the past eight years we had no place we could call home.

That night coyotes barked in the distance. It had been years since the Apaches heard the high-pitched yips that prairie coyotes make on a moonstruck night. It made the old people smile.

CONGER

One day, Harry and I drove from Lawton, Oklahoma, to Rush Springs. We found the probable location of the railroad depot, where the train had stopped in 1894 and let off the Chiricahua passengers. It was on the east edge of town in a shallow valley across from a park and cemetery. What was missing (this upset Harry) was a sign, or plaque, or marker indicating the historic significance of the spot. This was the place where the Chiricahua Apache, after an interval of eight years, officially returned to the American West.

As we rumbled along in Harry's pickup, he spotted some unusual features on the horizon. The time was early spring, and the Oklahoma sky was smeared with thick, pasty clouds. Turkey vultures sailed overhead; lark buntings fluttered from shrub to shrub; meadowlarks trilled in melodious voices.

"We got to take care of that," Harry said, grumbling over the fact that there was no marker indicating the spot at which the Apache had stepped down into their new life in the west. As we drove we kept looking to the west, but not even Harry with his extra-keen eyesight could discern the rocky, sloping outline of the Wichita Mountains. Granted, the Wichitas were a pale echo of the mighty Chiricahuas, but they were mountains nonetheless, with their own mystique and stories. Harry guided the pickup from one right-angled country road to another, following a tight, geometric, westerly path, so different from conditions in 1894 when his father, wearing brand-new shoes purchased from a store in Alabama, had ambled across a trackless prairie to his new home. Harry's smooth face glowed with the flush of discovery. It was always that way when he followed his father's footsteps for any distance.

Fort Sill, although built as a bulwark in defense against Indian attack, had little of the conventional fortress about it. Unlike Fort Marion in Florida, there was no moat or parapet or embattlement bristling with cannon. The buildings were not connected to form a stockade as were most other western forts. It was a pleasant military village, facing a common square, on all sides of which were stone buildings surrounded by lawns and gardens.

WATSON

Our first winter at Fort Sill was difficult. The Army provided wall-sided tents for each Apache family. Each tent had a small wood stove to heat the interior during the long winter nights. Every day I went out to collect wood for our own fires and the fires of the old women who didn't have anyone to gather wood for them. Another of my jobs was to carry water to the tents of the elders who needed it, as well as for my own family.

The Apaches were allowed to camp on both sides of Cache Creek, which ran through the middle of Fort Sill. We stayed there, under the trees, for two years, living in tents provided by the Army. Later, the Army built houses for each family. Eventually, twelve family groups of Apaches resided at Fort Sill in twelve separate villages or "clusters," each cluster presided over by a headman. The houses consisted of two comfortable rooms, with a breezeway in between and one or two windows in each room to provide additional ventilation. A post-and-wire fence circled each compound.

Once a month the Blue Coats doled out rations to the Apache prisoners: coffee, sugar, rice, beans, flour, and slab bacon. I liked to watch the soldiers measure out each of the items. One day a soldier said, "Hey, kid, I want you Apaches to give out your own rations. You think you're smart enough to learn how to do that?"

I didn't know how to read or write, but I knew where the mark was on the scale for the rice, beans, and flour. "Yes, I can do that," I heard myself say. The soldier showed me a thing or two about measurements, then turned the operation over to me. I don't know how long it lasted, but I began to give out rations, making a heavy mark on the scales for the three items: a small mark for the rice, another mark for the beans, a big mark for the flour.

Apaches don't like rice. It reminds them of white maggots. We took the rice allotment but refused to eat it. Apache women walking home carrying their monthly ration of rice would punch a hole in the corner of the cloth sack so the rice would fall through the hole and spill to the ground. By the time the women got back to their houses, the rice was gone.

We settled in. One of my first jobs was working with Old Man Gooday in the Officers Mess Hall at Fort Sill. I must have been nine or ten. I did a lot of different chores, but mainly I washed dishes. I was too little to serve plates full of food, but big enough to suds dishes. The hot, soapy water wrinkled the tips of my fingers. I rode my horse to work, and after my work was done I rode home. My mother Tah-Tzil-Toey always told me, "Don't ride too fast." Our house was located a half-mile west of the grove of trees next to the present-day H.E. Bailey Turnpike, where an American Legion Post stood until burning to the ground a few years ago.

My route took me across Medicine Creek, which always rose after a heavy rain. Medicine Creek was a powerful place, full of spirits; I was always respectful when I went there. When I was unable to cross the creek, I rode my horse to the railroad bridge, tied him there, and walked across the bridge the remaining half-mile to the mess hall. Some people heard voices when they were near Medicine Creek. One time I got off my horse and lay down in the grass a few feet from the water, when suddenly I was pelted by a rash of pellets spit out by some creature that lived in the water. I got on my horse and rode out of there. We all had stories about Medicine Creek.

As soon as the Chiricahua arrived at Fort Sill in 1894, the Army began to talk to them about the kind of land they would occupy when they were no longer prisoners of war. We assumed that we would be extended our own reservation in the same way the Comanche and Kiowa had been. In addition, those tribes generously offered to give us extra land that they had available, which made us feel positive about the future. We could see the potential, especially concerning cattle raising, of the land around Fort Sill. In theory at least, the Chiricahua had been promised a permanent homeland. A kindly officer named Hugh Scott was our liaison with the Army about this matter. At first, he seemed to be on our side, but then something happened. Behind the scenes, the Army reneged on its offer, citing the need for additional military installations to keep the country battle-ready for any emergency. (Such as putting down another Apache uprising!)

On January 9, 1902, the 29th Battery of the U.S. Army Field Artillery arrived at Fort Sill. The idea that Fort Sill might be converted to an artillery center began to take hold. In the summer of 1905, six more batteries arrived and took up permanent residence.

CONGER

Harry told me that Indians have trouble understanding white people. He says Indians look you in the face when they speak to you; white people look at your shadow. Part of the whites' uneasiness, I think, has to do with a lingering fear of the fighting prowess of the Chiricahua Apache. Geronimo never surrendered to the Blue Coats; neither did many other warriors. When the Spanish–American War broke out in 1898, the majority of troops stationed at Fort Sill were sent to Florida to be part of an American invasion of Cuba. With Fort Sill devoid of defenders, rumors ran wild that Geronimo and the Chiricahuas intended to rise up and attack the fort. Even when he was well into his eighties — for as long as he was alive — Geronimo kept the Blue Coats on edge. Despite the calm, placid, avuncular image he projected the last few years of his life, the White Eyes always dreaded that he was on the verge of bolting from the reservation and heading for Mexico to burn and pillage.

That simply wasn't the case. The Apache were tired of fighting and wanted to settle down on their own reservation and make it productive. But the Army wouldn't let them; all along there was a military and political faction in the American government that had no intention of giving the Chiricahua their own reservation, certainly not at Fort Sill and maybe not anywhere else. For various reasons, the land that rightfully belonged to the Apache became too valuable to turn over to them, even though it had been promised to them as part of the deal they struck with General Nelson Miles when they lay down their arms in 1886.

Geronimo died in 1909. His death brought no change for the Chiricahua people. The citizens of Arizona did not want them to return, and the U.S. Army did not have anything to offer them. Instead of providing the Chiricahua with a valid economic base by which they could support themselves independently of any government handouts, the U.S. administration threw open the surplus land to white homesteaders. The effect was devastating. Once again, the Chiricahuas were cheated out of land that was theirs. Instead of occupying a stable, contiguous land base where they could maintain and nurture their traditional way of life, individual tribal members had to settle for modest allotments of 160 acres, barely big enough to support a single family.

I was asleep in my bed on the second floor of a carriage house located on a busy street in St. Joseph, Missouri, my hometown. This was perhaps six or seven years ago; I'm not exactly sure.

In the balm of a deep sleep, something compelled me to open my eyes. There's a wall on that side of the room separating the bedroom from the living room. A door at one end provides access to both sides. The door was shut. As if by command of a fussy stage director the wall wasn't there, and in the gloomy gray light I could see every object in the living room: couch, coffee table, work desk, French doors leading to the stairs that slanted down to the ground floor of the carriage house.

Was I asleep? Was I awake? I couldn't tell. It was all so dreamlike, fuzzy and precise at the same time, hostile and brooding.

Even without my glasses, I could see all the furnishings in the room. Along the windowed south wall of the hybrid carriage house/garage—constructed of Georgian brick in the 1930s—I saw what looked like a black, sticky chunk of tar seeping into the room over the tops of the south-facing walls.

I wasn't scared; I was curious. I was seized by a sudden desire to find out what it was that was attempting to creep so stealthily into my house. The substance was black and slick looking; it slipped nimbly through a crack at the top of the windows facing out on the backyard. From my point of view, as I sat up in bed, it resembled a kind of viscid blob, glistening in the crepuscular half-light that bathed the interior of the room.

And then I knew. A flash of energy blazed through my body like an electric shock. Slowly, silently, the gooey substance (about the size of a standard bath mat) commenced to cross the room, slipping along the ceiling with the undulating grace of a manta ray. I went berserk. I started screaming at the intruder, a foul spate of obscenities: "Get out of here, you bastard! You rotten no-good mother-fucking piece of shit! Get out! Get out!"

. . . and found myself suddenly awake standing beside the bed, screaming my lungs out, pointing and wailing, punching the empty space over the bed with my puny fists. The wall between the rooms was back in place and my view of the living room was sealed off. I had awakened myself with my cries. Fortunately, I was alone in the room. My screams had torn through my throat with the shrill urgency of a siren.

Two weeks later, I was diagnosed with Parkinson's disease.

My wife came home around five the afternoon Darrell and I took acid so many years ago, when we had all those squirrely visions. Darrell was asleep in an apple tree in the backyard, wrapped in a hammock knotted at either end to a stout branch, swaying in the light breeze. He'd played a gig the night before with the three-piece ensemble he regularly jammed with at the downtown clubs. He was bushed, and it took the combined effort of Betsy and me to get him down from the tree. He seemed to be sleeping so soundly, I hated to wake him up.

"Darrell," I murmured.

His blue eyes popped open. He seemed to see all the way through me, as if I were nothing more than a mass of vaporous steam. A large vein on the right side of his head pulsed like a garden hose. His cheek felt warm and rubbery.

"I better go," he said in a hoarse whisper.

"Have a cup of tea first," Betsy suggested.

"Yes . . . lovely idea."

A while later I was in my little office off the kitchen scrawling abstract polymorphous figures with magic markers, one after another, as fast as I could manage, on the pad of drawing paper I kept at the ready. It was something I liked to do when I was loaded. The ease with which the figures came to life on paper was euphoric. It was like a Rorschach test, with floating blobs culled from the depths of my psyche, bubbling to the surface — of interest to me, of interest to my wife, maybe of interest to a student of psychology. What did they mean? A breakthrough of sorts; in place of the rigid brain cramp that usually hobbled my efforts to externalize my feelings, it was as if I suddenly learned how to let go and stuff started pouring out. Bizarre, twisted, warped, like images from a gothic novel by Horace Walpole or "Monk" Lewis. I'd always wanted to be a cartoonist, but I had no drawing skills. I know I was blocked in many areas of my life: stymied, thwarted, stunted. Too polite to ever declare satisfactorily just what it was that was on my mind.

Later that night, in bed, Betsy said sweetly to me, "Did you have fun with Darrell today?"

The expression soured on her pretty face. "You sure scared the hell out of me. Imagine coming home from teaching school and finding you and your buddy trashed out of your skulls. It looked like a pair of rats had entered your bloodstream and were eating anything they could find."

I knew what was coming. *Maybe I should get her some flowers*, I thought, *or a piece of jewelry*.

A look of desperation gnawed at the edges of her face. I wasn't easy to live with. "It's all about you, isn't it?" she said. "How far you can go?"

"I'm afraid so," I replied, and I rolled over and pretended to fall asleep.

So went life in the 1960s. For some of us.

WATSON

I must have been about eleven or twelve when Mother got the coughing sickness (tuberculosis) and was forced to remain indoors. My sister Maggie stayed with her. I helped by carrying wood and water and doing other chores. Mother's soft brown flesh turned dry and dark, and she became pitifully thin. Gradually she got sicker. Her breathing became raspy and harsh. You could hear her a long way away. She could hardly get out of bed and walk across the room. The fever would come and go, leaving her face wet with perspiration. The sickness sapped her strength. She could barely raise her head off the pillow to swallow some hot soup.

An Apache medicine man named Tocalanny tried to cure her. He sang and prayed each night for four nights, but it was too late for him to help her. We should have asked him earlier.

Gradually Mother lost her appetite. She was unable to get out of bed. She died early one morning in 1905. We buried her in Beef Creek Apache Cemetery on the grounds of Fort Sill.

I can still hear her telling me to "slow down your horse, you are riding too fast!" I remember her helping me cross Medicine Creek near Four Mile Crossing, one time when the water was too high for me to wade through. She threw a rope that I grabbed and tied around my wrist. I swam, she pulled, and I got to the other side okay. She was a brave and courageous woman.

Many of the Apache children taken by the Army to be educated at the Carlisle Indian Boarding School died there and were buried in Pennsylvania. A few children returned to their families in Alabama with the coughing sickness, where they died and were buried at the Mount Vernon Barracks.

The legendary woman warrior Lozen died at the Barracks and was interred in an unmarked grave. Lozen was as good in battle as any male warrior. She was a crack shot; she rode her horse with skill and daring; it was said that she could detect the presence of the Mexicans or Blue Coats merely by sniffing the air. Even Geronimo was impressed.

After our move to Fort Sill, still more of our people died of pneumonia and tuberculosis. We seem to have brought these diseases with us from Florida and Alabama.

Several members of our family (many young children including my half-siblings) died after we moved to Fort Sill. A boy named Larry (my half-brother) and a girl named Mary (my half-sister) both died from the same disease, tuberculosis or "coughing sickness," that took our mother. My older sister Maggie Fun died within a year of our mother from the coughing sickness she contracted while taking care of her.

My mother Tah-Tzil-Toey got together with Lawrence Mithlo in 1894; they had my sisters Violet and Mary. The only father I knew when I was a boy was Lawrence Mithlo. I called him "father." My sister Violet was born at Fort Sill in 1900. We went to stay with our aunt Tsis-tohn after our mother died. Aunt Tsis-tohn was good to us. She said, "I will take care of you now and when I get old, you can take care of me."

I liked being around my aunt. She had so many stories to tell about the old days when the Apaches lived in Arizona.

Before she married Lawrence Mithlo, Tah-Tzil-Toey was married to the warrior Fun, who rode with Chief Naiche and the warrior

Geronimo. Fun told my mother many stories about fighting in Arizona and New Mexico. Fun died in Alabama and was buried in the National Cemetery in Mobile, Alabama, under the name Lanny Fun, although his given name was Larry Fun.

Lawrence Mithlo met and later married Dolly Perico. Dolly and Isabel were the daughters of Warrior Perico, who rode with Chief Naiche and Warrior Geronimo. I remember Warrior Perico; he and I were prisoners of war at Fort Sill, where we worked together as cowboys, hauling hay and fixing fences and herding cattle.

CONGER

The late 1880s was the time of the Ghost Dance. Indians all over the West greeted the appearance of this mysterious ceremony with jubilation. From tribe to tribe the fever spread, ignited by a "Christianized" Paiute Indian from Nevada named Jack Wilson. One day Wilson slumped to the ground in the throes of a vision. He saw all the Indian nations come together, and to the steady boom of a drum, on quick, mincing steps, they began to dance in a circle. The message that emerged from Jack Wilson's mouth was simple: The grim fate of extinction that American Indians faced could be reversed, and instead of disappearing as had the buffalo, the Ghost Dancers would lead them out from their hiding places into a new world flush with fresh grass. Best of all, there were no White Eyes in this new world. "Come together in a circle," Jack Wilson said. "Join hands, and to the steady thump of a drum you will emerge into the light of a new day. The White Eyes will be gone. The world as we have known it will be covered with sweet new grass. Birds will crowd the sky. The thunder of charging buffalo will be heard from every direction."

Jack Wilson: a convert, dressed in lace-up shoes, derby hat, a three-button suit bound snugly across his chest and plump tummy. Charlatan/sage. Doofus/seer. An ordinary man bearing an extraordinary statement. "My message is simple," he said. "Take pride in who you are. Don't hesitate in your dedication and resolve. Have faith in the Old Ways. Observe our rituals and ceremonies. Honor your elders and kinfolk. Dance 'til you fall down, then dance some more. The world as you knew it will be restored."

Everywhere he went he drew huge crowds. Old people and young danced and danced until they dropped like brittle leaves in an October wind.

Such talk, especially from a lowly "digger" Indian, enraged the White Eyes. Soldiers in western forts were put on high alert. The Ghost Dances went on, flaring up in secret places. Military officers, consulting over glasses of whiskey and wine, composed their faces into somber masks. Didn't these people realize that they were finished as a race? Two more generations and they, like the buffalo, would be wiped off the face of the earth. Better in the long run that they accept one of the Christian sects, representatives of which arrived almost daily from churches back east. There were plenty to choose from.

But inexplicably, with the fury of a brush fire, the pagan gospel continued to crackle and roar. There was abundant kindling to feed it: squalor, poverty, hunger, oppression. The appearance of a native messiah was infuriating to the whites. Could it be possible that an Indian savior had actually arrived who had the power to return the earth to the lush bounty of the Old Days? The dance continued to surge through the West like a fiery comet. It was a giddy time and it affected all the people, but especially the Plains Indians: Comanche, Kiowa, Arapaho, Lakota, and Cheyenne. The military finally took action with vindictive wrath, along a remote creek in South Dakota called Wounded Knee, where 300 Lakota men women and children were slaughtered on a frosty day in late December 1890. The hope and promise of the Ghost Dance melted away in the bitter wind.

The Reformed Church in America was an important institution for the Chiricahua Apache. When Ulysses S. Grant became president in 1868, there was a movement on the part of some influential people to try to indoctrinate the Indians into the white man's religion. It was felt that persuasion could be as valuable a civilizing agent as coercion, and very quickly the reservations in Oklahoma and all over the West were inundated with missionaries of every denomination, Protestant and Catholic. The Reformed Church was one of the major groups to embrace this movement. Some of the Apache went to the school established by the Church there; others, who had accepted the white man's faith, attended the Church's services. The complex, located on the Fort Sill grounds, consisted of several buildings, including an elementary school, orphanage, laundry, church, and camp-meeting tent.

The Reformed Church held regular services for Indian people. By this time (circa 1895) there were many more Apache people who understood English from having attended the Carlisle Indian Boarding School in Pennsylvania or the Riverside School in Anadarko, Oklahoma Territory. They became interpreters for the Apache people; they helped conduct business between the Indians and the U.S. government. The Fort Sill church had three full-time interpreters: one for the Apache, another for the Comanches, a third for the Kiowa. The congregation sat in a separate section under a big tent. The preacher spoke to the congregation in English, using interpreters to deliver the message.

In the early 1900s, there was a great deal of worry and concern among the Chiricahua as to what was going to happen to them. As time went on, it looked less and less like they were going to have their own reservation. Fort Sill was on the verge of being converted into an artillery proving ground. Surplus land that should have been deeded to the Apache in fee simple was thrown open for settlement to white homesteaders. It was a tense and difficult time.

I need to speak to Melvin. I'm having health problems and I need a spiritual and psychological boost. A healing ceremony of some kind. I wonder if Harry could arrange it with his younger brother?

I haven't mentioned this to Harry. He's aware of my maladies. I enjoyed robust health until a couple of years ago when I was diagnosed with both Parkinson's and prostate cancer. Harry and I are about the same age. I'm sure he understands my desire to be singled out for a blessing ceremony. I need something for my soul, a spiritual kick in the ass to restore my energy and hope.

I need to get to know Harry and Melvin better. I've been to the doctors; I'm taking the pills; I but I need something else, validation of a different sort to restore my poise and balance. I have grown sadly out of whack with myself, mired in the miasma of a creepy sickness, a slow fizzling of the nervous system, one nerve at a time, pop-popity-pop-pop Parkinson's, a dirty, crippling disease. But I can't just ride up to Melvin's door shouting a friendly hello and expect him to pat me on the head and say, "Okay, Honcho, you're cool. Let's get started."

Indians are innately polite. They don't like to raise their voices in order to be heard. They don't like to disappoint anyone, especially themselves. They want to do what is right, correct, and cosmically viable. Anything else involves losing face, and losing face — losing your balance and integrity in the mad scramble of life — is one of the worst things that can happen.

HARRY

A band of Comanche in a war party toiling on foot across the empty grasslands met up with a band of Kiowa. This was back in the time when there were no towns or railroads. Nothing in this immense grassy space was nailed down. Everything was in flux: tossing, turning, tumbling in the capricious wind.

The Kiowa were in wretched shape: poor, ill clad, and hungry. They were clearly unable to defend themselves against attacks from hostile tribes. This was back in the time before the acquisition of the horse. They knew and the Comanche knew that if they didn't get some assistance, they were all in danger of dying. "Can you help us?" their headman asked his Comanche counterpart.

There were only two courses of action the Comanche could take. Either we killed all the Kiowa and put them out of their misery. Or we invited them to join us.

So that's what we did. We opened our ranks and let them come in.

The Comanche and Kiowa have been allies ever since. Even though we tell jokes about them.

WATSON

I was a young man around twenty-four when I married my first wife, an Apache prisoner of war named Phillipa Tooisgah, at Fort Sill. She was fifteen or sixteen, a dark-skinned girl, with lovely eyes and a strong jaw. We lived in Chief Chihuahua's camp, north of Medicine Creek. We were married less than eighteen months when she fell ill with the coughing sickness and died in 1914.

I remained at Fort Sill until 1914, an important year for the Chiricahua Apache. That year all prisoners of war who wanted to remain in the Fort Sill area were released to live on Comanche and Kiowa land allotments. The majority of these allotments were located around the town of Apache, Oklahoma. My father and stepmother, Lawrence and Dolly Mithlo, built a house two miles west of Apache, on a Comanche allotment. My aunt Tsis-tohn and I got an allotment near Hatchetville, a small community northeast of Apache.

I tried to join the U.S. Army in time to serve in World War I but was turned down. Instead, I went to work for a white man named Mr. Stewart, who owned a café in Apache. I did a little bit of everything for him: cooked, washed dishes, swept up at the end of the day. It wasn't uncommon for me to work from twelve to fourteen hours a day. I had no car to carry me home to Hatchetville, so I stayed with Lawrence and Dolly at their house in Apache. They had five children, which made things crowded when we all had to sleep on the back porch.

Mr. Stewart had a daughter named Marie. She was a tall, thin, white girl who loved to talk and ask questions. Back then I smoked — hand-rolled cigarettes, flavored with Apache tobacco. Marie wanted to smoke, too, so I rolled one for her and soon she was smoking with me. We got to be good friends and enjoyed each other's company.

One day we up and got married. Our son Roy Delano Mitchell was born on September 11, 1922, in Little Rock, Arkansas. Roy's mother had moved there as it was where most of her family lived. I knew I had to find a better job than cooking hamburgers to support my family so I took a job driving a truck, which meant I was gone from my family for days and sometimes weeks at a time. This caused a lot of friction between Marie and me, and our marriage broke up. Marie took Roy to Ardmore, Oklahoma, where her family lived, and enrolled Roy in a Catholic school under the name of Roy Gray. He had a hard time adjusting to the strict rules laid down by the priests and nuns. Meanwhile, Marie married a car dealer from Ardmore. The man took good care of Roy and treated him like a son. After graduating from high school, Roy enrolled at Oklahoma State University in Stillwater, where he earned a Bachelor of Science degree. Following that, he worked as a civil engineer with the U.S. government in Mississippi.

Years later, Roy told me about his experiences in the Catholic schools in Ardmore. His mother put him in the school to get rid of any trace of "Indian-ness" that might indicate his race. Roy learned how to fight when somebody called him an "Indian half-breed."

Roy was a tall, dark-haired young man with honey-colored skin. He got tired of the abuse at the school and ran away. When he was brought back, he told the nuns, "I want to go see my father." They whipped him, and Roy ran away again. The priests and the nuns beat him so many times he had trouble walking.

Roy told me he hated the school and everyone in it. He began to exercise to build up his strength and stamina. He lifted weights to build his muscles and began to plan how he was going to escape. He filled a knapsack full of food and water. After several months of training, he was ready to make his break.

One night a Catholic-school sister came into the room to make her regular bed check. Roy stood in a shadow against the wall. As the door opened, Roy stepped out of the dark. There in front of him was the sister who had beaten him so severely. Roy hit her in the face and knocked her over a bed. Then he ran out of the building and disappeared. He never went to another Catholic school again. He never went to a Christian church again because of the way he had been treated.

I met my present wife, Lavina Chasenah, as she was carrying water for her family. This was sometime in the early 1930s. She was Comanche. She and her sisters carried water each day from the pump to their house. I took one look at her and knew I had to meet her. So I volunteered to pump water for her family and help carry the buckets to her house.

Lavina was strong; she had the long, muscular legs of a runner. She was tall and pretty, younger than me by over twenty years.

One day I went to meet her at the pump when she was there alone. At that time I was renting a room from Ralph and Mary Pewewardy. In the 1930s, Ralph and I worked for the Civilian Conservation Corps (CCC), repairing roads and bridges in that part of Oklahoma.

I talked with Lavina and invited her the next day to my house to eat fry bread. I make really good fry bread. Back then, I liked to entertain the ladies by making them fry bread. Lavina came, and I found out she was a Comanche from the Penatuka ("Honey Eaters") band. She had two sisters, Pearl and Beauty.

It was 1932 and the Great Depression had put a clamp on the economy. Everyone was having a hard time. I think it was easier on Indians because we never had anything anyway. We knew how to get along with very little at our disposal. Sharing was an important feature of our culture.

Lavina and I were married by a justice of the peace in Chickasha, Oklahoma. In 1943, I went to live with Lavina and her grandmother Mahkanarsy. We raised the following children: Roy Mitchell, Kenneth Chasenah, Vincent Redbird, Leatrice Pewewardy-Jay, Harry Mithlo, Eugene Mithlo, Elvina Mithlo, Lavera Mithlo, Bill Mithlo, Melvin Mithlo, and Mary Tabbytite.

We had been married for about a month when one day Lavina said to me, "You made fry bread for me before we were married, and now that we're married you don't make fry bread for me anymore!"

In 1889, the Kiowas and Comanches came to Fort Sill to meet with the Apaches, starting an intertribal friendship that has lasted for many years. For generations the three tribes have gathered at Four Mile Crossing at Cache Creek to talk, play cards, race horses, and dance. Indians, especially the Apache, love to dance. Apache men gladly paid girls from other tribes to dance with them. The Apache have social dances called the Back and Forth Dance and the Round Dance. When the Comanche and Kiowa girls came to camp, we would dance the night away. We held them in such a way that we faced one another so we could talk as we danced back and forth across the floor. This was a good way to become acquainted with one another. Because the dances were properly chaperoned, not only young people but married couples could dance with other mates without anyone becoming suspicious or jealous.

The Apaches could always tell when the Comanches were in the vicinity. They gave off a distinct woody aroma similar to that of sage or cedar. All Comanches radiate this pleasing scent.

Later I learned from my Comanche wife that the fragrance was used as a kind of protection against evil. It was made from crushed purple flowers (horsemint) that grew in wet patches in the spring; the Comanche called this pungent fragrance "Indian Perfume."

In 1900, the United States Congress ratified the infamous Jerome Agreement, which opened the Kiowa and Comanche Reservations to white settlement. Fort Sill came under the control of the War Department. Within two years of the fort's change of status, military officials decided that it ought to be retained by the federal government as an artillery proving ground. It was then that the Chiricahua realized that they would not be allowed to keep the homes they had been promised. Once again, our people had to pack up and find another place to live. Once again, we were victimized by the White Eyes' greed for land.

CONGER

How Indians became cowboys is an important story. The Chiricahua Apache were very much involved in this momentous historical shift.

In the early 1910s, the federal government decided the Indians had too much land, so they looked for ways to relieve them of it. First the Comanche, then the Kiowa. According to the treaties they had signed, each adult in the family was to be given a 160-acre plot. (The government said it was a 160-acre plot, but actually it was much smaller than that, sometimes amounting to little more than 80 acres.) The same held true for the Apache. But 160-acre plots, whether in the Fort Sill region or out on the Mescalero Reservation in New Mexico, weren't big enough to grow major agricultural crops such as wheat and corn. The scarcity of water in both places was a chronic problem; without it, the people couldn't raise a profitable yield of anything.

The Comanche's and Kiowa's historical experience as buffalo hunters enabled them to shift easily into cattle raising; the same was true of the Chiricahua and other plains Apache. Lacking an adequate, tillable land base, the Chiricahua were forced by circumstances to become cowpunchers. To ensure ownership of the 160-acre allotments newly bequeathed to them, the federal government decided to sell off the Apache cattle herd that the tribe had painstakingly accumulated over a span of several years, so that families could use the proceeds to buy additional Indian land. This was especially helpful to the one hundred or so Chiricahua Apache who opted not to move out to Mescalero; their share of the cattle money was used to purchase surplus land from the Kiowa and Comanche so they could reside comfortably in the Fort Sill region.

Preparations for the all-important cattle sale began on January 3, 1913. Three months later, over five thousand branded head had sold for around $235,000, a healthy sum then parceled out to each Chiricahua not inclined to move farther west to the Mescalero Reservation (located in south-central New Mexico). In the process, however, their primary economic asset — the cattle herd — was depleted.

Nobody knew much about Mescalero. It was heavily wooded; the winters were long and cold. Many of those who wanted to remain at

Fort Sill were fed up with once again having to step into the unknown. They didn't mind living at Fort Sill. The Army made the choice all the more complicated when they told the Chiricahua in 1914 that they were no longer wards of the state. After nearly twenty-seven years, the Chiricahua remaining in Oklahoma were relieved of their hard-luck status as prisoners of war.

Not even the Confederates following the end of the Civil War or the German – and Japanese-American POWs at the end of World War II were as shabbily treated by the U.S. government as were the Apache after their wars with the Blue Coats. None of the other tribes that had waged war against the U.S. Army — Kiowa, Comanche, Shawnee, Arapaho, Modoc, Nez Perce, Lakota, Northern and Southern Cheyenne — were held in captivity for more than five years. They either had new reservations established for them or were returned to reservations in the general region from which they had been originally removed.

WATSON

I worked with cattle at Fort Sill, taking care of them year round. We fed the animals during the winter; when the ponds froze, we broke the ice so they could drink. It was hard work, but I liked being outdoors.

One winter day when I came in from work, Aunt Tsis-tohn said that she was going to make some work shirts for me. She was a good shirtmaker, and she made a new shirt for each day of the week. My cowboy friends liked the shirts and complimented me on my good taste.

I had many jobs as a cowboy. Each day I checked the fences for breaks. When I found a loose wire, I mended it. I counted the cattle in my area during my daily rounds. One day when I was feeding the cattle, I cut the wire on a bale of hay. The loose end of the wire snapped back, hitting me in the eye. I knew I'd been hit hard. I didn't know if the wire had cut my skin or my eyeball, but I did know that I was in a lot of pain. I covered my eye with a kerchief. When I saw blood, I got back on my horse and rode to find the foreman. He laughed as he inspected the wound. "You're okay," he said. "Just keep the kerchief on your eye. The injury won't keep you from working. Now get back to work!"

I didn't like the way he spoke to me. We had a few more words, and I turned and walked back to my horse. He grabbed me by the jacket and stopped me. I took the walking stick from my saddle and hit him on the left side of the face. I don't know where he went after that, but I went home. I thought the tribal police might show up at my door, but they didn't. The injury caused the sight in that eye to become cloudy like a cataract. Eventually I lost sight in that eye. Having only one eye was difficult, but I adjusted to it.

My son, Harry, can see like an eagle. There's something to be learned here: When we are hurt we have to reach all the way inside ourselves to find the hook that holds it all together. We need to cling to that point; it defines us not only as individuals but as a people. We have to deal with what comes our way, bad or good, with dignity and restraint. We are the children of Ussen. Ussen will guide us. Ussen will show us how to survive.

The Army would not allow us to assemble in groups for the purpose of having fun. For example, we liked to get together to play cards and dance. But every time we did somebody would snitch on us. Typically, the Army overreacted. They assumed that we were getting together to launch a raid into Mexico. Those days were long gone, but our reputation as warriors always made the Blue Coats uneasy.

In 1908, tuberculosis was rampant in the Apache camps. The Army didn't want us to dance or get together in big groups for fear of spreading the disease. They didn't want us to share smokes or eat anything together.

A respected Chiricahua man named Jason Betzinez turned out to be the snitch. He was a ferocious warrior when he was young, but when he got older he became a kind of fuddy-duddy. He thought he was doing the right thing when he tattled on the Apaches, telling the cavalry where they were and what they were doing. A squad of Blue Coats dutifully mounted up, rode into their camps, and drove the people back to their houses. The Apaches watched out for Jason Betzinez and kept track of where he was at all times. The women were especially helpful. They let Jason know that on a particular night the Apache men would be, say, playing cards at Martine's encampment. A group of riders took off in the direction of Martine's camp. As soon as Jason saw the riders go off, he ran and told the Army. When the troopers reached Martine's camp, there was nobody there playing cards. They played this trick on Jason several times until the Army stopped listening to him. Betzinez also tried to ban the Mountain Spirits Dance, which did not endear him to anyone.

I planted a garden each year for my family. What we didn't eat I sold for cash. I sold watermelons all summer to the Comanche and Kiowa camps along Medicine Creek. I had melons, corn, cucumbers, and other fresh produce.

Enoch Smokey and I became good friends. Enoch was a Kiowa man, who lived in Verden, Oklahoma, with his wife. In the summer, they traveled in a large horse-drawn wagon and camped at Fort Sill for months at a time. Smokey loved to hear Apache songs. He loved to sing them. It didn't matter where we were or what time of day it was.

Smokey got to be friends with the older Apache prisoners of war: Eustace Fatty, Geronimo, Chief Naiche, Jason, Chatto, Old Man Gooday, Perico, Kawaykla, Mangus, Loco, Chihuahua, and Walter Louie. Whenever I met up with Smokey, he'd start singing an Apache song. He liked the spontaneous way the songs shifted into different pitches and rhythms. He liked the way they seemed to explode with energy. Plains Indian songs are characterized by the same hard, steady beat from start to finish. Apache songs are much more subtle and engaging.

"I had a good time in the old days," Smokey said.

The Apaches had been at Fort Sill for many years but, other than a few allotments, they still did not have their own land. There was talk around the fort that the government was giving land away to people who put their names on a paper for a lottery drawing. This was the summer of 1901; all anyone had to do was write his name on a paper and be chosen to get land. The land was from the government, free of charge.

Several Apaches got together and signed up for the land. I went with Eugene Chihuahua, Walter Louie, Harry Perico, and Lawrence Mithlo to the office at Fort Sill to apply for the drawing. When we approached the desk to sign our names, the man sitting there, a pinch-faced bureaucrat with skin as white as an onion bulb, said, "This land is for white people. You Indians gave up this land for white homesteads."

"When did we do that?" we asked in disbelief.

"A while back."

"How far back?"

"Far enough back to make you ineligible. Sorry."

So we were not allowed to apply for the land drawing because we were Indians!

The Indians had given the land to the White Eyes to settle on, and we didn't even know it was ours! I sure wish we could have gotten our names on that list. We might have had a chance to own some real land. The Army said that because we had been prisoners of war at Fort Sill, we had to get special permission before we could do anything.

They had us coming and going.

Geronimo died on February 17, 1909, of pneumonia. He liked to drink, especially tiswin, a potent Apache potion distilled from fermented corn. This particular night in February was cold and damp. At Geronimo's urging, his grandson Eugene Chihuahua obtained two bottles of local whiskey. It wasn't easy. Eugene had to be careful. If he got caught he'd go to jail.

Geronimo was eighty years old, maybe older. He and Eugene rode around for a while, pulling on the whiskey bottles. At one point, Geronimo fell off his horse. Eugene tried to pick him up and put him back in the saddle, but the horse wouldn't stay still long enough for Geronimo to get back on. Instead, the two men proceeded to drink more whiskey and passed out on the cold ground. Toward dawn, they were drenched with an icy rain. Geronimo was feverish and coughing when he woke up.

Somehow, Eugene got him to the Fort Sill hospital. The doctor examined him and said he had pneumonia. Eugene got a man to ride over to Geronimo's house and tell his wife. Word passed quickly; people gathered outside the hospital, waiting, listening. He lingered a few days. Somebody was always at his side. He knew he was mortally ill. He asked his nephew Asa Daklugie to make some medicine for him. He took the medicine that the white doctor left him. Neither did any good. He faded in and out of consciousness.

Feelings about Geronimo ran strong. Some people hated him, others revered him; he was too powerful a personality to bring everybody together. His presence in any situation was polarizing. Asa Daklugie was the son of Chief Juh and Geronimo's beloved sister, Ishton. When Asa was born his mother was sick for four days. Juh, her warrior husband, was raiding in Mexico. Geronimo, a skilled medicine man, pulled his sister through the birthing process. At one point, he thought she was going to die. He went up to Mount Bowie and prayed. Ussen heard him and said, "Go back to your sister. Both she and her child will survive. You, Geronimo, will live to be an old man. You will die a natural death."

It was as Ussen said. Daklugie was born and Ishton recovered. Geronimo was wounded at least eight times in various parts of his body, sometimes severely, but he didn't die in a shoot-out.

The Army buried him in a cemetery on the west bank of Beef Creek at Fort Sill. Many former Apache prisoners of war attended the funeral. Chief Naiche spoke to all the people in the Apache language. He said that as Apaches they had to keep on living; if too many of them — especially those of childbearing age — died, they might disappear as a people.

That was something we always worried about. It could happen that one day we would wake up and realize that there simply weren't enough of us left to carry on with our way of life. That's why in battle we had to be sure that not too many of us were killed. The Apache had a different idea regarding warfare: A successful raid was one where there were no casualties. Each warrior, male or female, was indispensable. We had to be careful and smart. There weren't that many of us left.

It is important to remember that my people have never told everything they know about themselves — their culture, their history, their spiritual life. We believe that as Apaches we must keep this information to ourselves, especially for our children in order that they will continue to identify themselves as Apaches.

A group of men including me was chosen to remove the body of Geronimo from his gravesite in the Fort Sill cemetery and rebury it in the nearby Wichita Mountains, north of Lawton, Oklahoma. In addition to being a warrior, Geronimo was a medicine man, and it was important to the Apache people that his body be reburied in a secret place away from the depredations of the Blue Coats and souvenir hunters.

I had to stay late at work the evening we reburied Geronimo. I didn't complain about having to work late, although I hurried out to meet the other men as soon as I finished. At Chief Chihuahua's camp a woman came up to me and said, "They have taken his body away."

I hurried to catch up with them. The night was cold and dark. The rolling landscape looked as if it were glazed with ice. The elders had chosen a moonless winter night so they would have plenty of time to do what they had to do. A rotating team of young men did the actual digging. They were strong and could endure the cold weather. The elders worked out a system whereby no one would know for certain where the body was reburied. No one in the group would ever say anything, even speculatively, as to where that spot might be.

In a straight line it's about five miles from Geronimo's Fort Sill gravesite to the closest Wichita Mountain. After digging him up, the young men carried the remains on a stretcher at a trot, each man clutching a corner. Five miles was a long way in the bitter darkness. When they got tired, they dropped out and headed back home. Other men took their place. No one questioned what was happening; it had all been carefully worked out. The men who reburied him, young and old, are all dead now. They died knowing that no white person could ever steal the body and cut off the head. Geronimo's spirit was free to roam where it wanted.

CONGER

Maybe it was an omen. Soldiers stationed at Fort Sill in the early days tried to relieve the boredom by playing endless games of baseball. The enlisted men liked to meander over the hills east of the post, catching horned toads, tarantulas, and other creatures. They carried them back to the fort, showed them off, prodded them into fighting each other, making bets as to which was the better killer.

One day while rolling stones down the face of Medicine Bluff, the soldiers uncovered a rattlesnake den at the base of the cliff, a few feet above the waterline. Reptiles in large numbers slept through the winter, rolled together for warmth in glistening coils. The soldiers extracted over a hundred torpid rattlesnakes, which they killed and skinned. Snakeskin belts and hatbands became the fashion of the day for both officers and enlisted men at Fort Sill.

WATSON

Once I had the job of roping coyotes for the Army so the officers could entertain themselves. By 1910, Army officers had hunted all the coyotes out of the Fort Sill region; there was nothing left but foxes. A couple of Apache cowboys and I would rope the foxes and bring them in so the officers could enjoy a live hunt. I would ride down a fox, rope him, and stuff him in a sack. Then I would hang the sack from a tree and go catch another fox.

One day I caught four foxes. When I went back to pick them up, I found that they had clawed a hole in the sacks and escaped. The coyotes and the foxes taught me something: I never chased after another animal so other people could harm that animal or run it to death.

My aunt Tsis-tohn married an Apache man named Sam Houser while they were both prisoners of war at Fort Sill. They had no children together, but Sam had children from a previous marriage.

One day in 1911, Sam and I rode to Medicine Bluff. There wasn't anything going on in the village that day, so we decided to see what we could stir up. Medicine Bluff is a sheer, vertical, granite bluff that faces north and overlooks Medicine Creek, a deeply spiritual place.

We were to meet some other young men at the bluff, and as soon as they arrived, we sat down for a smoke. Sam was eager to climb so he crossed the creek and started up the bluff. He climbed halfway up the sheer rock cliff and came back down. A few soldiers appeared just as Sam was making his way down the cliff. They wanted to know if we thought they could climb to the top of the cliff. They wanted to make a bet that no Indian could possibly climb to the top. Sam bristled. He told them he could climb it without difficulty.

Sam was halfway up the face of the cliff when a soldier started to climb up after him. Sam had no problem reaching the top of the cliff. The soldier got stuck high up on the gray rock face and couldn't go up or come down. He shouted to the other soldiers to get help. By this time, Sam was down off the cliff, lying on his back near the water, smoking a cigarette. The other soldiers had to get a bunch of ropes to rescue their buddy. They called us a lot of bad names, but we didn't care.

From springtime through autumn, Apache cowboys broke horses for the Army. We were bold and daring riders, and although the horses kicked and bit us, we liked working with them. We taught them to stop, back up, and pull loads. We took turns breaking them. Now and then one managed to buck us off, but that only made us better riders.

Each year in the spring and fall, Apache cowboys had a calf roundup, where we branded the calves and gave them their shots. We cut off a few bull calves' balls, which made good eating after a hard day's work. Indian cooks knew how to cook for Indian cowboys, and we were grateful and slipped them extra money for their efforts.

There was a white man from Texas named Burke Burnett who sold horses to the Army. He liked the way I handled horses and cattle. I could look at a herd of horses and pick the best ones. Something about the way they moved, the sleek muscles rippling under their smooth coats. He asked me if I'd be interested in taking a job as a cowboy on his ranch in Texas, south of the Red River. He offered me a house, horses, a wagon if I took the job.

Needless to say, I wanted to go to work for Burke Burnett.

Burnett checked with the Army about the job offer, and they told him that I had been a prisoner of war and that I could not be released to go to work for anybody. Sadly, I missed a good job with an opportunity to earn a good living. I've often wondered where I would be today if I had taken the job with Burke Burnett in Texas.

Another time, I shot my best friend for stealing. I was cooking breakfast for myself; the coffee was boiling, the eggs and bacon frying, the biscuits baking. I had just put the bacon on the table and was reaching to get a knife when I heard a noise and turned to see my dog with his jaws clamped down on the bacon, dashing out the door, heading south. I grabbed the rifle above the door and shot him in the side. He whimpered a little and died. I picked up the bacon, washed it, and continued to make my breakfast. After I ate it, I went outside and buried the dog.

It is taboo for an Apache to eat or kill a pig. We don't eat javelinas (a type of wild pig) because they eat snakes, and it's taboo for us to eat snakes. My mother never ate pork.

One day a soldier told me that ordinary pigs raised by white farmers were kept in a house, cooled with fans, elevated off the floor on platforms so they couldn't wallow in their own waste. The farmers fed them a special mash mixed with oats, corn, and wheat. I liked the taste of bacon even though I know my mother would not have approved.

We Apache love to race horses. We had a racetrack at the Fort Sill parade grounds, just south of the horse corral. (Today, that spot is at the intersection of Interstate 44 and the main entrance to Fort Sill's Key Gate.)

We liked to race not only against our own people but also against Comanche and Kiowa riders. Many people mistakenly believe that the old horse corral was the location of old Fort Sill because of the narrow windows that make it look like a stone fort. Old Fort Sill was located at the top of the hill, west and north of the horse corral.

Clay Domeah was a good Apache cowboy. He worked in the fields, but what he liked best was to race horses. One day—I believe this was in 1911 or 1912—six horses lined up to race. When the bell sounded, the riders jumped on the horses as they were galloping practically at full speed. The cowboys waved their arms as they raced toward where I stood near the corral gate. As the horses neared the gate, the riders pulled back on the reins to get them to slow down. Clay Domeah slowed his horse, but instead of stopping, the horse slid on his back hooves and fell backward on top of Clay. The saddle horn hit Clay in the center of his chest. The weight of the horse crushed Clay's heart. He was lifeless when we reached him.

CONGER

It was my fifth or sixth trip to Lawton. It took all day to drive from Kansas City, Missouri, to the Wichita Mountains. Along the way, I brooded on our project to write a book about Harry's father.

I didn't think we had enough material to write a proper biography. However, Andy Wilkinson, the Texas Tech University Press series editor, wanted me to add my own experiences to the mix.

"What's the point of that?" I riposted. "The book's not about me; it's about the Chiricahua and Watson Mithlo." I felt that Andy was giving me conflicting instructions. Harry and I had already written three drafts of the manuscript.

"Next time you go through it, just add your thoughts and feelings," Andy advised. "It'll give us a different perspective."

"What about the dance?" I said.

"I think you ought to write about it from a ground-level point of view. From the point of view of the dancers."

"Ground level . . . "

"Yes. Definitely. You down there with the dancers."

"But Harry's told me more than once that there's stuff here that he can't tell me and I can't use."

"Well," Andy chortled, "I suppose there is stuff here that's classified. But you go ahead and put it down and we'll see what we can keep and what we can't."

Were Andy and Harry in cahoots? I was confused. Up to this point, I had functioned as little more than a hired gun. That was all right; I was grateful for the work and all the good stuff I was learning. Still, I didn't quite know what my role really was.

Juanita Pahdopony, Harry's wife, is a petite, pretty woman, a Comanche, with warm brown eyes and a passionate interest in art. The walls of the house she shares with Harry are covered with paintings she has collected over the years or painted herself.

Currently, she is an assistant professor at Comanche Nation College. She and Harry have been married for a dozen years. Each has grown children from earlier marriages. One night, talking about Harry, she said, "He asked me out after seeing me at his family's sweat lodge. He said to someone, "I seen her coming across the prairie grasses and she looked like a strong woman."

She said, "I've been married several times, and Harry's the one I've been waiting for."

WATSON

In 1913, the Chiricahuas were finally permitted to leave Fort Sill and move to the Mescalero Apache Reservation in New Mexico. The Army reneged on its promise to turn over the land at the fort to the Apache, Comanche, and Kiowa tribes so they could live on a proper reservation. Instead, the Army decided to expand the boundaries and convert the fort from a cavalry post into a field-artillery training installation.

Not all the Chiricahuas wanted to move to the Mescalero Reservation. Those like myself who wanted to stay at Fort Sill were eventually placed on Kiowa and Comanche allotments; these allotments rarely amounted to more than 160 acres each, hardly enough land to provide a viable base for a serious economic enterprise such as farming or cattle ranching.

After my release as an Apache prisoner of war in 1914, I was eager to see the world. The home I knew at Fort Sill was no longer my home. The houses that the Apache prisoners lived in were now the property of the U.S. Army. Once again, the White Eyes got us from both sides. If we wanted to be released from military custody, we had to give up our claims to all property at Fort Sill.

Those Apache prisoners of war who did not move to the Mescalero Reservation but chose to remain in Oklahoma lived at Fort Sill until they secured an allotment. They were not free to go unless they had family to stay with or an allotment was purchased for them.

I received eighty acres west of the little town of Hatchetville, Oklahoma. My aunt Tsis-tohn also received eighty acres. Lawrence and Dolly Mithlo received an eighty-acre allotment located west of Apache. They built a small house and we all lived together in that small house until we built houses of our own.

The day of departure for many of the Chiricahua for the Mescalero Reservation was a sad day. We had grown to like it at Fort Sill and we were reluctant to move yet another time. The Army had lied to us so much in the past that we were doubtful that our new home on the Mescalero Reservation would be as comfortable as what we had become accustomed to at Fort Sill.

The day of departure, April 2, 1913, was a day of sorrow, with much weeping and wailing. Once again, families were broken up; once again, the Army was sending us into the unknown; once again, we had no idea what was going to happen to us. The Army forbid us to take our dogs along, but when the train arrived at Mescalero and the doors opened, scores of dogs poured out of the cars, howling and crying.

The White Eyes who lived around the Mescalero Apache Reservation were fearful that the appearance of the Chiricahua in New Mexico would spark an outbreak of hostilities. As long as he remained alive, Geronimo was thought by the White Eyes to be capable of raiding any place in Mexico or the American Southwest any time he wanted. Even before 1909, the year of his death, such fears were groundless. In the summer of 1903, Geronimo joined the Dutch Reformed Church (from which branched the Reformed Church in America) and was baptized.

Things had changed; the old warrior was no longer interested in robbing and pillaging. He willingly embraced a new life.

The only contest the Chiricahua engaged in upon arriving in New Mexico was a baseball game between the Indians and a Mescalero team of whites and Indians held in the town of Cloudcroft. The Chiricahuas blitzed the Cloudcrofters with a score of 22–2. The local newspaper noted in its account of the game that the "Fort Sill boys romped around the diamond and ran scores while some of the Cloudcroft boys were trying to put the ball somewhere — just where was not always plain."

"No one wanted to kill the umpire or scalp anybody," the article continued. "The game passed off pleasantly."

Meanwhile, back at Fort Sill, we all felt that the ball game was a good omen for the future. For the Chiricahuas who moved there, an era replete with unfulfilled promises, dashed hopes, and shattered expectations had drawn to a close. Only time would tell whether their removal to New Mexico had launched them on the long-awaited road to happiness, prosperity, and contentment.

My aunt Tsis-tohn and my sister Violet were part of the group that moved to the Mescalero Reservation. A year went by and I felt as if I had been left alone at Fort Sill. I missed our close family members and needed very much to see them again. My brother Eugene Chihuahua had moved to Mescalero, and I missed him too. (After Chief Chihuahua died, Lawrence Mithlo's brother married Chief Chihuahua's widow. So Eugene was as though a brother to me.) I didn't have enough money to buy a train ticket. It was too far to walk. So I saddled up my favorite horse and rode out to New Mexico.

WATSON

I left Fort Sill early one morning with ten dollars in my pocket. I brought along a few pans, a fork and spoon, a bag of horse feed. That first day, because I knew it was going to be a long trip, I walked my horse for the first twenty miles. Each day I found grass and water for him and firewood for me. I cooked my meals each evening early enough so I could enjoy the last glimmer of western light as the sun slipped below the horizon. I always camped away from any creeks or ponds to avoid being harassed by the water spirits.

At night I heard the sounds of coyotes and other animals. One night I was awakened from a deep sleep by a crunching sound. I moved my eyes, rolling them back and forth, trying to locate the source. I turned my head to the right and saw a doe feeding on the grass next to my head. I closed my eyes and went back to sleep.

The country back then was nowhere near as settled as it is today; there were fewer fences and roads, fewer people and houses. I crossed many creeks and long stretches of dry grasslands and stopped in small towns along the way to buy horse feed and candy bars.

Someone once asked me if I felt alone when I was by myself out there.

"No," I said. "I felt comfortable and at ease. Apaches are never really alone even when they are in the middle of nowhere. I see the shadows of my ancestors. And of course there are the mountain spirits."

I looked like a Mexican cowboy. The white people in the small towns did not know that I was Apache. I wonder what they would have done had they known. Probably thrown me in jail, or lynched me. It's hard to believe how much people feared the Apaches back then. To them we were scary — a danger, a scourge, a force. A few people spoke Spanish to me, which I understood. They wanted to know where I came from, where I was going, what my name was.

After a few days, the terrain changed from rolling hills to mountains, bigger than the ones around Fort Sill. It took me several weeks but I finally arrived at Mescalero in the late afternoon, footsore and happy.

The majority of Chiricahua Apaches lived in the mountains in the community of White Tail, about twenty miles north of Mescalero. The Mescalero didn't want the Chiricahua Apaches to live too close to them. I believe it was because of their fear of the potent medicine the Chiricahua possessed. Geronimo and the other warriors could do amazing things when they had to. One time when the cavalry caught up with the Apache, close enough to fire at them, Geronimo cast a spell that made the Blue Coats think the creatures passing in the dark were nothing more than a herd of bawling cattle.

I stayed in Mescalero for several months, working in a logging camp. I had a friend named William Peso, and we made a good work team. Peso was born in the Guadalupe Mountains, near present-day Carlsbad. As a boy he had ridden the Plains with Chief Natzili, who led an eastern band of Mescaleros on raids into Mexico. Peso got his name for his fondness for the Mexican silver coin.

To keep myself well fed, I did a lot of logging. It was hard work, dangerous, but I liked it. I was young and cocky and quick on my feet.

One day a chain broke on a trailer piled high with logs, and they rolled off the trailer and tumbled downhill right at me. "Watch out! The logs!" Peso yelled. Fortunately, I was able to jump to the side and avoided getting crushed by the logs.

There were occasions when we had to spend the night in a logging camp, and during those times I used to cook for the loggers. I was a good cook, having learned a lot from Mr. Stewart, owner of the cafe in Apache, Oklahoma. One afternoon during a slack period, Peso and I were walking through dense mountain brush. A fellow we knew stood on a hillside above us, and from this vantage point he was able to see down below for quite some distance. "There's a bear headed right toward you!" he yelled. Peso and I hollered as loud as we could and jumped up and down, flapping our arms. The bear ran off in another direction.

One day we noticed that the bottles of vanilla extract, which we used as flavoring for making cookies, were disappearing. It seemed like each time we checked there was less and less vanilla. A few days went by. Two men from our logging camp became sick and a third died. They'd been stealing the bottles and drinking the extract.

Whenever I went into White Tail to shop and do business, I spoke English to the clerks. Some Apache children heard me one day. "Hey, here comes the white man!" they hollered. When I answered them in Apache, they were dumbfounded. I understood not only what they were saying but what the clerks were saying!

I missed my friends and family back in Oklahoma, so I decided to go back home. Mescalero was interesting, but the winters were long and cold. I took the train to Lawton. The trip lasted several days. I slept most of the way and woke up as the train was passing through the Wichita Mountains. It felt good to see those modest little mountains. My heart felt warm. *This is a good place*, I thought. *There is goodness all around me here.*

Joe Ivens was a young man in his twenties when I met him. He played baseball with George Asepermy and stayed with Grandma Mahkanarsy, who took him in as though a son. She lived across the field from George in a big house with a screened-in porch and a detached barn. Joe had his own bedroom on the third floor. He could see the baseball field from his window.

We became good friends. We were both Apaches. He was a White Mountain Apache from Fort Apache, Arizona Territory.

Joe was a good baseball player. He was a smart hitter and fast on the bases. No matter which Apache team he played against, his team usually won. Joe and his teammates could lay down bunts with surgical precision. They perfected sliding into home plate without getting tagged.

Years later, a car drove up to our house in Apache, Oklahoma. My wife Lavina went outside to see who it was. The driver, a young woman, said that her grandfather in the passenger seat was looking for his best friend, Watson Mithlo. It was Joe Ivens. He had driven back to Oklahoma from New Mexico to visit the old home place in Apache where he had once lived with Grandma Mahkanarsy.

Joe wanted to see how much the town of Apache had changed from the time he had left. The stores, gas stations, and streets had changed very little, but the old Levite store, where almost anything could be bought, was missing from its street-corner location. When he saw the old home place, Joe started crying. The big house where he had once lived had been reduced to four rooms. Grandma Mahkanarsy died in 1957 and was buried at Cache Creek Cemetery.

Joe's granddaughter took care of him after his wife died. Joe died in 1982 and was buried at Fort Apache, Arizona.

Henry and Lena Archilta owned a dance ground west of Boone, Oklahoma. The dance ground was close to a creek shaded by big trees and was popular with all the area Indians.

In 1974, a group of dancers came from Mescalero to dance for Henry Archilta. Eugene Chihuahua came with them. It was good to see him again. We lived so far apart, it was hard for us to get together. Eugene planned to stay for the weekend. The Comanche, Kiowa, and Kiowa Apache people came to Boone to watch the dancing and listen to the Apache songs. Everyone, even non-Apaches, liked those songs. They were full of surprises.

Eugene met a Comanche woman named Maude from Apache. The young couple danced the Apache Round Dance and the Apache Back and Forth Dance all night long. These two dances are special social dances for the Apache people.

When the dance was over, Eugene left with the group and returned to Mescalero. He wanted to see Maude again. He wanted to marry her.

Maude had two daughters, Mabel and Marie. They did not want their mother to marry Chief Chihuahua's son. Whenever Eugene went to see Maude, the daughters kicked up such a fuss that he finally changed his mind about marrying their mother. That was too bad. I wish Eugene had married Maude; then we would have lived closer together and seen each other more often.

Eugene stayed with me and my wife Lavina in Oklahoma for a month. He met another Comanche woman named Hew-wau-ney from Indiahoma. She had been married to a man named Hosetosavit, and they had six children. Eugene went to visit Hew-wau-ney and soon they were going places together. Eugene asked her to marry him. She accepted, and in 1983 they moved to Mescalero to live in White Tail.

Eugene and Hew-wau-ney didn't have any children together. One of Hew-wau-ney's sons drank too much, and it caused such problems for the couple that they eventually separated. Eugene remained single for a long time after that before he met a woman he wanted to marry.

Her name was Jeannie. She was a small, polite, quiet Apache woman. She had children from a previous marriage. Eugene met Jeannie in Mescalero; after they married, they moved from White Tail to Mescalero to a house near the old Apache feast grounds. They were a great couple. Eugene finally found the happiness he had wanted for so long.

Eustace Fatty was a fellow tribesman and a former Apache prisoner of war at Fort Sill. He left there in 1913 to live on the Mescalero Apache Reservation. His father, Old Man Fatty, had a Mountain Spirit Dance group while he was a prisoner of war. This group was given to Eustace when Old Man Fatty died. Eustace and I were long-time friends. I knew his family like my own.

Eustace wanted to give me his dance group, but when he died his sister Mattie (Mary) got the group, which she also offered to me. I did not accept the dance group because my brother Eugene Chihuahua had already given me his Mountain Spirit Dance group, and I had accepted.

Old Man Gooday, a Warm Springs Apache, also wanted to give me his dance group (ceremonial garb), but I couldn't accept it. Old Man Gooday told me that his son Robert had come and asked to borrow the regalia, but he had never returned it. To the Chiricahua Apache, the Dance of the Mountain Spirit is a ritual dance with ancient origins. It is a dance of blessing and healing to the Chiricahua people.

Sometime in the 1950s, I visited Eugene Chihuahua in Mescalero; he took me aside and told me about the dance group he wanted to give me. He wanted to make sure that I did the right thing with the dance group. He wanted to make sure that I took care of it, because in return, in the Apache way, it would take care of me. We talked for many hours in front of the chicken shed behind his house. The dance outfit was carefully stored in his barn. Eugene wanted to be sure that I used the Mountain Spirit group the way it was supposed to be used: as a powerful instrument for the welfare of the people.

In the spring of 1958, Eugene was admitted to the Mescalero Indian Hospital. I made plans to drive out to see him. After Eugene was released from the hospital, he made several tape recordings of his Apache Round Dance Songs, Back and Forth Songs, and Blessing Songs for me to use. He encouraged me to make a new dance outfit for the following year's feast on the Fourth of July in Mescalero. He asked that I share the songs with my sons and that they learn all about the dance group and carry on after he and I were gone.

I spent an entire year getting the new outfit ready for the feast. A family that sponsors a feast usually hires a dance group. Each year some family would hire Eugene to dance and he would ask me if it was okay. I would always tell him, "Okay, let's dance!"

I loved to dance as much as he did. Dancing kept me close to the earth. I always felt better afterwards. It made me feel Apache in every part of my body.

CONGER

I'm concerned about the book; there's still no title. I'm worried that it's not dense enough, lacking texture and detail. These Apaches are not the most voluble people on the planet. Small talk is not their forte. A shrug, a wag of a finger, or a blink of an eye are enough to communicate with a fellow tribal member. Unfortunately, these subtleties pass me by. I need things to be out in the open and animated, so I can view them from a three-dimensional point of view.

I think Harry believes he has given me enough material to work with. I don't think he has. Writing is a process of selection and distillation. I like working with a lot of primary material. I like to choose my words from a big pile of verbiage. I like to ferret my style out of a sloppy mass of phrases, excerpts, notations, non sequiturs, dashes, telegrams, arcane marginalia and fragments. My attitude is basically one of inspired gluttony: at this point, early on, the more the better. I need to wallow in the messiness in order to locate the silver lanyard of the narrative arc.

Harry's not bothered by this. He gets it right the first time. He says what he needs to say and no more. I have to dig and drill and excavate truckloads of crummy ore before I can discover a few worthwhile gems. All this leads me to conclude that there are two kinds of writers in this world, the vulcanists and the sedimentarians. The vulcanists spew forth the words in a single draft. The sedimentarians (myself included) practice their craft in the manner of the laying down of a coral reef, over millions of years, line by line.

WATSON

Upon my arrival in Mescalero at the start of the Fourth of July Feast in 1965, I found that my dear friend Eugene Chihuahua was in the hospital. The feast was only a few days away, but Eugene assured me that he just had a bad cold; otherwise, his health was fine. He asked if the new dance outfit was ready, and I assured him it was.

I went to his house to unpack the new outfit and found that there were some men inside the barn getting the old outfit out of storage. I didn't want any trouble with them, certainly not with Eugene in the hospital. He and I made plans to take the old outfit into the mountains and put it away so that no one would ever know where it was. We planned to start the New Year with a completely new dance outfit.

The next day I went to visit Eugene in the hospital.

"Well, did you dance good?" he asked.

"Yes," I said.

I didn't want to upset Eugene by telling him about the men I had seen rooting around his barn. I lied to him because if I had told the truth, I was sure he would walk out of the hospital and confront them. He might have sent the tribal police to remove them from his barn. I thought, naively, that the situation would take care of itself. I now regret that I did not take the old dance outfit with me to Oklahoma five years earlier, as Eugene had suggested.

In the spring of 1966, I received a letter from Jeannie Chihuahua. The entire contents fit on a single sheet of paper. She confessed that she had done wrong "by selling the outfit." She knew that the dance outfit belonged to me, but she went ahead and sold it anyway. The letter was signed "Jeannie Chihuahua."

Later that year I got word from relatives in Mescalero that Melford Yuzos was trying to solicit enough money from the Mescalero people to buy the Chihuahua outfit from the tribe. I also heard that Carius Naiche, granddaughter of Chief Naiche, told Melford that the Chihuahua dance group belonged to me. Carius Naiche was not going to give money to anyone to buy a dance group. Dance groups can only be "given" to another person; they can't be bought and used as if rightfully belonging to the purchaser. The older Apaches knew this, and so did tribal chairman Wendell Chino. It was clear that Eugene Chihuahua had given the Chihuahua dance group to me. It was also clear that Jeannie Chihuahua had sold the dance outfits.

Eugene Chihuahua and I went back a long way together, to the time when we were both prisoners at Fort Marion. Melford Yuzos had neither a relationship nor a connection of any kind to the dance group or the dance outfit.

The following copy of a two-page letter, composed by my family and signed by me, was sent to Chairman Wendell Chino of the Mescalero Tribe sometime during the 1980s. The letter explains the ritual passing on of the dance outfit. The Chihuahua dance outfit bears the star trademark that distinguishes it from other dance groups.

> To Whom It May Concern:
>
> I am writing this statement to my people and to your office [the office of Wendell Chino, Mescalero Apache Tribal Chairman] concerning the dance group of my brother, the late Eugene Chihuahua.
>
> Eugene got his dance group from Old Man Martine. It is the custom of our people to give their outfits to a worthy individual to keep and maintain. Eugene was given the dance group in order to preserve the dance. The dance was given as a blessing to the Apache people.
>
> Before Eugene became the sole owner of the outfit, Old Man Martine gave the outfit to Eugene and Ralph Chee as joint owners. After Ralph died, Eugene became the sole owner of the outfit. In 1963 Eugene gave the dance outfit to me [Watson Mithlo] as a way of blessing the people and preserving its safe keeping.
>
> In 1962 Eugene told me to make a new outfit. The old outfit was to be put away and the new outfit was to be used when completed. That same year, Eugene asked me to take the old outfit home to Oklahoma. Instead, I left it with him. In 1963 he asked me if I could dance at the annual feast in July. He said he wasn't feeling well. I took charge of the group for my brother that year. In 1964 Eugene asked me if I could dance during the feast. I danced and sang for the group that year.

In the spring of 1965 I got a call from Eugene. He said he was sick and needed to talk to me. I went to Mescalero to be with him. We talked a lot about the past. We talked about old friends such as Eustace Fatty, Block Shields, Alton Peso, Rufus Sago, George Martine, Sam Kenosi, and John Mast. While I was in Mescalero, Eugene spoke into a tape recorder in our native tongue, telling me that the dance outfit was mine. He gave me all the songs for the outfit—dressing songs, crown dance, round dance, back and forth, morning songs, and blessing songs. He wanted me to teach my sons these songs so they could carry on the celebration. After a short stay of only a week, I went home to Oklahoma.

In 1965 I returned for the Fourth of July feast. The new outfit was ready to be used for the feast. Eugene wanted the group to dance during the feast. I went to the house to get the old outfit, but Melford Yuzos and some others were there in the barn. I didn't say anything because I didn't want any trouble between the families. The next day Eugene asked me if we danced good. I told him we danced real good. But we didn't dance. I didn't want to upset Eugene by telling him that the outfit was being used by another group.

After the feast, I returned home to Oklahoma with the new outfit. Eugene Chihuahua died on December 16, 1965. I went to his funeral and talked with his wife, Jeannie. Eugene always called me his brother; we were cousins and we knew each other from our days as captives of the U.S. Army in Florida, Alabama, and Fort Sill.

Out of respect for Eugene I didn't dance for four years. In the spring of 1966, Jeannie Chihuahua sold the old dance outfit. After she sold the outfit, she wrote me a letter stating that she had no right to sell the outfit. "It belonged to you," she said. "Can you please forgive me? Watson, I did you wrong by selling the outfit."

Then I heard that Melford Yuzos had bought the old dance outfit for a price and was asking people for financial support for the purchase of the old outfit.

I told everybody that the dance outfit would take care of itself. Later, I heard that it had set itself on fire and was destroyed. I never said anything after that. The old outfit took care of itself. It had that power. If it didn't like the way it was being handled, it could self-destruct.

Melford Yuzos is dressing dancers and using the star pattern under false pretenses. In doing so, he shows no respect for the past owners or the present owner. What right has a man to start his own group by buying or making an outfit for the purpose of dancing or for show? If this was so then our traditional outfits are meaningless. Our customs and traditions are strongly rooted in the spirituality of the Apache people. Anything else is bad medicine.

I see now why Eugene Chihuahua wanted me to take the old outfit home so there wouldn't be any trouble. If I had taken the outfit home, the situation would be solved. In 1984, I turned the new outfit over to my youngest son, Melvin Mithlo. Today, he is in charge of the Chihuahua group.

I want all the Apache people in Arizona, New Mexico, and Oklahoma to know that Eugene Chihuahua gave me the star to wear; he also gave me the medicine that goes with the dance group. I have represented the Chihuahua dance group well, and I am looking forward to going to Mescalero to dance.

Now and in the years to come anyone or any organization that asks Melford Yuzos to dance for them is making a big mistake.

This way was sacredly given to me, and that is the way I intend to follow.

Respectfully,
Watson Mithlo

There are some things that Indians don't mess with. Good medicine can turn bad if it's mishandled or misappropriated. Certain objects and people are more numinous than others.

A tree, splintered by lightning, glows with a serene radiance. What makes this happen? Is it accidental, or is there a guiding hand? The crackling bolt suffuses each splinter with a magnetic glow. Touch any part of the tree and you will feel a jolt. The world is charged with its own dynamic, which feeds and fuels our spirits and bodies. To obtain this vision, to luxuriate in it, to make it work for the people who deserve it most. Is this what it means to be Apache?

CONGER

Harry Mithlo brought me directly from the motel in Lawton to the dance grounds located on the outskirts of the rural village of Apache, Oklahoma. A warm, early-autumn sun beamed down through a fleecy cloud cover. Harry's pickup was packed with supplies purchased in Lawton for the women working in the ramada under the shade of the brush arbor at the south edge of the dance circle. They swarmed the vehicle as it bumped to a halt, emptying it of food, paper plates, plastic forks and knives, cans and jars and sacks of stuff to eat and drink. No beer or alcohol of any kind. The dance ground was cut smoothly, with a turf-like feel to the grass, similar to that of a golf-course fairway. (Golf is Harry's favorite sport.)

He and I have been working on our book about Watson for three years now. At least a couple of years. I'm unsure what kind of progress we've made; we still seem a long way from wrapping it up. I don't know what the end is going to be, and I don't think Harry knows either. Still, I'm having a good time, learning lots about Apache culture and history, enjoying Harry and Juanita's company.

I like spending time with Harry. He maintains the same steady, focused, deliberate pace. He seems never to get rattled or distracted. He's an elder in the tribe, always in demand; he must serve on a hundred committees. As far as I can tell, he's more than just smart; he's strong, thoughtful, connected, always with the welfare of the people uppermost in his mind. Harry looks like a leader; he talks like one; he acts like one. People take notice when he enters a room.

The dance ground in Apache seems much bigger than it actually is. It covers a spacious circle half the size of a soccer field. "Tonight, when the dancers trot out to the fire, it will get really big," Harry says.

At the center of the spacious circle is a fire pit, around which, once it was dark and the fire had been lit, the Mountain Spirit dancers would perform their astonishing choreography. I opened the door to the pickup and slid down until my toes touched the ground. "Oh, look," a couple of women cooed at the entryway to the kitchen. "It's Harry and his friend." I had brought them several packages of American Spirit cigarettes, which I deposited in a rag pouch hanging from a wall in the kitchen. In return, Harry's sister Lavera gave me a slug of buffalo meat to sample. "We're taking a chance here," she says. "None of the food has yet been blessed by the medicine man."

Several tipis were already up when we arrived, including the one belonging to the Mithlo family, in which out-of-town guests will spend the next two nights sleeping on blankets and buffalo robes. I helped Harry erect a pavilion next to the tipi where people will sit during the dances with an unobstructed view of the fire and the dancers. An hour later I slipped into the tipi to listen to Harry and his younger brother Eugene tell Apache stories to a group of teenagers. The afternoon air was laced with the smell of sunbaked leaves, mixed with odors from the cook shack. People were slowly gathering on the premises for the annual Mountain Spirits Dance, scheduled to begin this evening at sunset. Harry was expecting a big crowd. The weather looked promising. "They trickle in one by one," he said. "Then boom! Before you know it, the place is full of Indians."

It was warm inside the tipi, comfortable, out of the wind that was yielding a chilly edge as the temperature dropped. I stretched out on a lush buffalo robe, eyes closed, in a state of total relaxation, happy to be there, happy to be with Harry and his family, happy that they were happy that I was there.

"This evening before the dance we'll have a Chiricahua feast for all the dancers and their families and guests," Harry said. "A major grub-fest to give us energy for tonight's festivities."

He looked at me, adding, "There are a few rules you need to know. There's no using proper names for anything for the next two days. We're all brothers and sisters for the time being. Also, there are no artificial lights. We cook everything over wood fires. Everything has got to be natural. One of the purposes of the dance is to make contact with the spirits."

Eugene looked professorial with his smoothly combed hair, flared up in a modest pompadour, thick bifocal glasses teetering on the tip of his nose. He lit a cigarette and eased into a story about Geronimo when he was being chased by the U.S. cavalry. An intense expression settled in the center of his smooth face. His dark eyes, magnified by the lenses of his eyeglasses, resembled a pair of polished nuggets. How many times had I sat with a native storyteller and listened to him or her recount a creation tale or a story about Coyote? At first, these stories seemed opaque to me and I had to listen carefully and ask questions to catch their drift. When you first hear them, Indian stories don't seem to be about much of anything; their meaning is deeply coded in familiar figures such as Coyote, who rampage through their oral tales with a freedom and vigor that could come only from a people who understood who the figures were and what role they played in tribal life. These figures carry the burden of meaning the stories have for their listeners.

Eugene and Harry must have heard these stories a thousand times. They don't seem to tire of them. Harry sat in a canvas-backed chair, eyes shut, hands folded primly in his lap, chortling at what Eugene was saying.

I struggled to pay attention. The buffalo robe radiated a comforting warmth. Eugene's voice was soft and steady, a melodious baritone that soothed my rattled nerves and brought my pulse down to a comfortable tick. It always takes a day or two to adjust my metabolic clock to the steady, quiet pulse one encounters in Indian-land. Life here seems more deliberate and focused. Yes, it's filled with strife and woe and hardship, but it also offers another dimension in which amazing things can occur.

We took a break while Harry and Eugene ran an errand for their sister. Alone in the tipi, I nestled deeper into the buffalo robe. A memory uncoiled like a strip of grainy celluloid through my sleepy brain. December, 1990. I was part of a contingent of walkers making a pilgrimage to commemorate the 100th anniversary of the Wounded Knee Massacre in South Dakota. There were twenty or thirty in our party, along with a sizable contingent of horseback riders; a cadre of monks and nuns from Japan; and a dozen sympathetic French and Germans, dressed in high-tech, cold-weather gear. The rest of us, a motley band of Indians and *wasicu* (white people) from disparate places such as Albany, New York, and Kansas City, Missouri, were dressed in cast-off clothing culled from Goodwill stores. The weather promised to be bitterly cold, and it was. One night when the thermometer plunged to thirty below, we took refuge in a barn on the farm of a compassionate white man. All day we had followed the path taken by a Miniconjou chief named Big Foot, as he led his people to a fateful rendezvous with the U.S. 7th Cavalry Regiment in a remote and little-known place called Wounded Knee Creek.

An elderly native couple from Canada occupied the stall next to mine. There was lots of straw, which they banked into a comfortable mound and over which they spread a dark, lustrous buffalo robe. They wiggled out of their sweaters and sweatshirts and patiently and laboriously rolled themselves into the robe. "I have some extra gear, if you need it," I said.

"We'll be fine," the woman said.

"I hear the temperature tonight is supposed to plummet to well below zero."

"The buffalo robe will keep us warm."

In the fading, ashy light her face was smooth and chamois-soft. I watched her as she ran her long fingers through the deeply textured nap of bristly buffalo hair that enveloped her. Her age I guessed as maybe sixty. Her cheekbones were high and prominent, her eyes an appealing green. I could barely discern the face of the man lurking under the robe next to her.

"We are Cree people from Saskatchewan," she explained. "We were down here a couple of years ago with a party of tribal elders looking to buy a small herd of buffalo from the Lakota."

The man raised up on one elbow. He had long white hair that spilled over his shoulders. "First-class buffalo," he said.

The woman smiled crookedly. "At one point we told the Lakota officials that we wanted to be left alone with the buffalo. The Lakota moved away from the pen, back into the trees, out of sight. There were maybe eight or ten animals we were considering. A small herd. A disease had devastated our own herd, and we badly needed replacements. The Lakota left us alone, and after a few minutes we found out what we needed to know. We wanted to make sure that the animals still spoke our language. That we could understand each other. So we bought them and took them back home, where they have worked out fine. We're here to support the Lakota. What happened to them at Wounded Knee in 1890 was unspeakable."

The next morning the woman and her companion were up and off before I opened my eyes.

"I think our guest is sleeping," Harry said as he and Eugene slipped back into the tipi.

"If we fell asleep in school," Eugene said, "we got our rumps switched." The memory seemed to amuse him. "Remember them teachers, Harry? Remember how mean they were?"

Harry let forth with a throaty, grumbling laugh. "They sure liked to whack us."

"Where'd you get this buffalo robe?" I asked.

"It's Melvin's."

Harry settled in the canvas-backed chair; almost instantly, his eyes relaxed into puffy slits. "Eugene," he said, "tell our friend about White Painted Boy."

"You told me about White Painted Boy the other day in the car," I said.

"You need to hear it again," Harry insisted.

Eugene lit a cigarette. "Ah, brother, you can't ever get enough of this stuff."

"Did I tell you about the time White Painted Boy and Dragon had a shoot-out with bows and arrows?" Harry asked. "Dragon shot first. He had four arrows in his quiver. They were made of pine and were twenty feet long. Well, that old Dragon took aim; just as the arrow left the bow, the boy made a funny sound and leaped into the air, whereupon the arrow shivered into a thousand splinters.

"Four times he did this, missing each time, prompting White Painted Boy to say, 'Dragon, you go stand over here. It's my turn to shoot.'

"Dragon scoffed. 'Your little arrows can't pierce the primary coat of my horns. And there are three more coats under that.'

"White Painted Boy then shot an arrow, striking the dragon in the chest. The next shot loosened another coat of horny scales, which clattered to the ground. Then another, exposing Dragon's heart.

"The boy fired his last arrow with true aim, piercing the dragon's heart. With a tremendous roar the dragon rolled down the mountain side, into the canyon."

Harry's voice quavered as he said, "Storm clouds swept the stony peaks, lightning flashed, rain erupted in dazzling sheets. When the storm passed, far down in the canyon, they could see chunks of the Dragon lying among the rocks. The bones of the Dragon can still be seen at that spot."

"The boy's name was Apache," Eugene added. "Ussen taught him how to prepare herbs for medicine, how to hunt, how to fight. He was the first chief of the Indians and he wore eagle feathers as a sign of justice, wisdom, and power. To him and to his people when they emerged into this world, Ussen gave homes in the Land of the West."

As the recitation wound down, Eugene's voice faded until it was barely audible. Harry sat in his chair with his arms folded over his chest, head down, staring at the bare, hard-packed floor.

A few minutes passed. Harry looked up. "There's only one creature left on earth from the age of the dinosaurs, and that's Bigfoot."

Eugene (a twinkle in his eyes): "Bigfoot? You don't say? Isn't that what Melvin heard the other day in his backyard?"

Harry chuckled.

Eugene explained that a few days ago, their younger brother Melvin heard five Bigfoot cries in a row, one after the other, pulsating from a nearby field, each lasting fifteen to twenty seconds. Everything went dead quiet. Even the yappy coyotes in the neighborhood fell silent.

Eugene fired up a fresh cigarette and puffed ruminatively. "Indians were the first people on earth," he declared. "There's nobody older than us, I don't care what the anthropologists say."

The expression on his face was darkly nuanced, reflecting measures of both pleasure and pain.

"Nobody goes as far back as we do," he continued. "We remember when we could speak with the animals."

"We see lots of strange things," Harry added. "It's in our blood. We're different from other people."

He rubbed his hand across his mouth. That's when I saw that the palm of his right hand had turned bright red.

I was about to say something when Harry said, "We share this stuff with each other, but not with outsiders. We don't tell anyone about Bigfoot, especially the cops. They think we're a bunch of savages, like the Apache scouts thought we were back in the bad old days when they chased us with the Blue Coats."

Harry: "These experiences are the only thing we have left that's totally ours."

Eugene: "Me and Harry have an aunt on the Mescalero reservation, who used to put out food for the Man, she claimed, that lived in the woods near her house."

I mulled this over. I was baffled and exhilarated at the same time. All this ancient, traditional, old-fashioned, hands-on magic in the midst of ordinary modern life with its electronic gadgets and television sets and pickup trucks. That's what makes it so extraordinary. Not only the magic, but the fact that that power—solace, empathy, vision; whatever you want to call it—is being passed on to the next generation. It is alive; it is a part of our world.

Eugene rose slowly to his feet. He wasn't as tall as his brother, but he carried himself with the same dignified bearing. His jaw was set, his expression furrowed. "There can't be anything negative for the next two days," he said. "This powwow is a blessing ceremony. We are here to heal and give thanks."

More people arrive as the afternoon drifts by, driving every kind of vehicle, jalopies and fancy SUVs. They put up their tents and tipis, unpack food, water, and soft drinks. No alcohol is permitted on the premises. The circumference of the dance circle is starting to look congested. Pickup trucks, piled high with logs and limbs, pull up to the north edge of the dance circle. By mid-afternoon there's a huge pile ten feet tall stacked in a tidy heap.

"What kind of wood is that?" I ask.

"Chestnut primarily," Harry says. "It burns hotter and slower than just about any other tree we can find in this part of Oklahoma."

I'm still trying to process the business about the Bigfoot in Melvin's backyard. Are these guys having me on, or is this really taking place?

"Harry, I don't understand something. I know there are plenty of Bigfoot sightings in the Pacific Northwest. But down here in the middle of the continent?"

"Shoot," Harry says. "Ol' Bigfoot likes to go south in the winter like any other snowbird."

I laugh. Good old Harry, yanking the chain of the gullible white boy.

"There's lots of Bigfoot sightings in and around Lawton," says Eugene. "There are white hunters that would like to see one, not to kill it they say, but just to look at it. We won't let 'em do that."

"How come?"

Harry looks at me carefully. It feels as if a solid wall of ice momentarily inserted itself between us. "'Cause they'd ruin it for everybody else," he says. "That's all I'm gonna say about that."

I still don't understand. But I keep my mouth shut.

Eugene: "There's a woman we know who had an encounter recently in the Lawton area with something she couldn't identify. She was walking alone on a remote trail in the Wichitas when she spotted a pile of bones. A voice inside her told her not to look up but to keep her eyes fixed on the trail. She kept hearing something but didn't dare look up. She could feel its presence. She could smell the foul odor wafting off its body."

The hair stood up on the back of my neck.

Eugene: "The granddaddy of them all was the 1947 Roswell, New Mexico, UFO crash. You know about that one. Everyone knows about that one. The night of the crash the Little People left the Mountain Spirit dances early and headed east toward the crash site."

"Were they the Little People?"

"Who?"

"The people in the crash. Were they sent here by the spirits to help the Apache?"

"Some people think the so-called 'space aliens' the military supposedly found in the wreckage weren't aliens at all. They were what we

Apache call the Little People. The gray people."

"So what did they find?"

"I don't know. Our dad wouldn't tell us. It was all very confusing. 'They're just like us,' he said. "'We're just little people ourselves.'"

"Were they the little people?"

"Maybe so."

"Why wouldn't he tell you?"

Harry looked off, his features composed in a fleshy mask. "I don't know," he said after a lengthy pause.

I went after him like a yapping poodle. Now was my chance. When Harry doesn't want to say anything he lapses into a ponderous silence. This time I was going to root him out.

"Why the secrecy?" I said. "Is it something you need to know? Is it something I need to know?"

Harry shrugged and looked away. A faint smile crinkled his lips; his big shoulders shifted away from his neck as he lapsed into a deeper silence.

I was confused, but maybe I was supposed to be. I can't believe he didn't know. Melvin had to know. Melvin knew everything.

I was aware that I was getting a little too bold and insistent, making it awkward for Harry and Eugene, putting them in an uncomfortable position. What did I need to know and what was it that they couldn't tell me? I decided to give it one more go.

We'd had a talk earlier about holy mountains and what they mean to the people who live in their shadows. I asked Harry about the significance of Sierra Blanca (White Mountain) located on the east slope of the Tularosa Basin, up on the Mescalero Reservation. Feeling cheeky, I then asked him the names of the four Apache holy mountains in the region. He stared back at me with an expression that made me realize that I had maybe overstepped the delicate line of restraint and good manners that held us together.

"Apaches don't tell outsiders everything," he explained. "The Comanches are instructed by their elders to make up something. Apaches are told not to say anything."

The wind curled and slithered around the canvas edges of the tents and pavilions, making them flutter like pennants.

At 4:30 p.m., we're standing in line outside the brush arbor waiting to be fed by the women who have been cooking all day. There must be at least two hundred of us, standing around with paper plates in our hands, talking up a storm. It's nippy out, but not uncomfortable. Harry asserts that when you put on a feast you not only have to feed everybody, you have to give them enough so they don't go away hungry. A few minutes later a half-dozen men start flailing with sticks on a big drum. Men, women, and children form a line in front of the drum and commence dancing in place in a joyful eruption of energy.

A handsome, dapper gentleman named Johnny Benitez—a Seminole and a great favorite of Harry and Juanita—appears. He wears a black vest, a necklace bedizened with polished orange beads, a serape draped over his thin, elegant shoulders, a white shirt with prominent French cuffs, a hand-loomed blue sash, a black belt spangled with concho buckles. He dances inside the circle with his six-year-old granddaughter. She wears a trim buckskin dress. A pearly white shawl covers her bare arms and shoulders; an eagle feather dangles from her hair. They make a lovely couple, delightful to watch. I have the feeling it's going to be an interesting evening. For sheer glamor and dramatic presence, few events can match an old-fashioned Indian powwow.

By 5 p.m., many of the young men who've been socializing quietly drop out of sight as the sun begins to crowd the horizon. The drummers continue to bang the big drum. The circle expands like the loop of a flexible lariat to include a dozen more dancing women and men.

In an hour, there are more dancers than drummers, moving vigorously back and forth, laughing in each other's faces and hooting. The powwow is beginning to catch fire. Dancers warble and cry out.

The fire master, hefting a heavy shovel piled with glowing wood chunks, staggers out to the pyre and carefully places the pieces in the hole. A wispy skein of smoke curls into the air.

Criers move around the dance area, calling people to supper.

At the entrance to the cook shack, we pitch into a tasty repast: buffalo meat, pinto beans, corn, spuds, salad, slaw, cake, cookies; we eat and eat until we can eat no more.

I sit inside the medicine tipi watching Melvin prepare the dancers. This is a very special privilege that I have been granted. Harry escorts me to the opening in the tipi facing east and hands me a pack of cigarettes. "Give these to Melvin," he says. "Tell him I sent you. That it's okay for you to be in there with him."

I did as I was instructed. The tipi was crowded with boys and young men getting ready for the dance. (Women do not dance with the Mountain Spirits.) A few sticks burned in the fire hole. The older boys, teenagers, strapping young guys, were dressed in tight-fitting regalia with greenish-gold symbols and solitary stars painted on their backs and chests. A couple of them had already put on their masks, which flattened their features so that it was nearly impossible to tell where their noses or eye sockets were.

The young dancers dart and wiggle between the big boys. Melvin corrals them one by one, and with a hand laid firmly on their shoulders, he draws the sticky brush across their pudgy backs and chests. For the most part the boys remain quiet and reserved; they are six or seven years old, blubbery, pubescent kids like so many others in the franchise-food world of southwest Oklahoma, except that at this moment they are about to be transformed into gods. Their eyes are dark and luminous, their mouths pouty and swollen, their bellies flabby and plump. Their flesh is so buttery it seems edible. The bigger boys take their time putting on their outfits. The camaraderie is good, with everyone helping everyone else.

That is until Melvin leaves the tipi for a few minutes, whereupon the little guys start to bicker and fuss; the older boys quickly silence them. I like that — discipline meted out by all the authority figures, not just Melvin or Harry.

I'm intrigued by Melvin. A burly man, with a pockmarked complexion, he wears glasses, smokes incessantly, gazes at me coolly and skeptically. "Who has Brother Harry gotten himself involved with this time?" I can almost hear him mutter. "What Anglo wannabe from the other world has he accepted graciously into the Apache fold?" There's something tough and pugnacious about Melvin — thorny as a cactus, he's not the type to back off from any sort of confrontation. He knows all the stories, all the secrets.

Later, back in the medicine tipi, Melvin applies the last bit of paint to the body of a little boy whose features, sheathed in a gossamer mask, have made him difficult to identify. Once the back and chest of the last little boy have been properly decorated, Melvin leans back and lights a cigarette. He stares evenly at me and says out of the blue, "White people don't have a clue about Indian spirituality. They keep living the same hurtful, destructive way. They don't know that it's really the Indians who are holding the whole thing together. We have been from the beginning, and we still are today."

Michael Mithlo, Harry's son, enters the tipi with an armload of dry sticks, which he places into the fire hole and ignites with a wooden match. A few minutes later the inside of the tipi fills with choking smoke, which functions, I presume, like a kind of smudge or elixir to purify the dancers before they emerge into the cool, breezy night. Togged out in close-fitting, body-length bodices, they chant a final, high-pitched prayer four times as they circle clockwise around the fire pit and exit backwards through a vent in the tipi wall.

"When they come out of that tent," Harry tells me, "they'll look like gods, even the little guys. The regalia, the headdresses, the masks, the sticks they carry in each hand. But it's more than just the regalia. It's how they carry themselves, the angle at which they hold their heads, the way they bob and weave, the cooing sounds they make, the way their feet skip lightly across the grass. They are not of this world, but they are."

I join the dancers outside on the rim of the circle that unfolds across the grassy dance floor in an elastic arc. Across the way a line of men ranging from teenagers to white-haired elders sits on a long bench, clutching drums and rattles and eagle-bone whistles. Just then, with no signal or cue that I can detect, the drumming begins. A surge of emotion rushes through my veins as the lead dancer steps into the circle and starts toward the fire in a stuttery trot, his body blackly silhouetted against the snapping red and orange flames. Halfway across, he utters a soft, whooping, dove-like coo. Reaching the crackling fire, arms extended like a swooping hawk, he veers clockwise around the pyre, shoulders squared, chin extended. The big boys move now with balletic grace, the little guys bouncing behind them on their small feet. The crisp October wind kicks up sparks that gush and swirl. I have never seen anything like this. The drums, the singing, the cool, invigorating wind, the snarling fire, the gnarly antlers poking from their skulls, the acrobatic shimmer of their lithe, youthful bodies, the musicians' voices meeting in chilling unison.

At the same time, the dancers from the Mescalero Apache Reservation in New Mexico, their chests, backs, and shoulders coated with a black, inky fluid, emerge from their tipi and glide deep into the dance circle to a chorus of high-pitched yips. The contest is on; for a few hours, the best native dancers in this part of the world go joyfully head to head.

Led by the fire master, the wood crew piles on fresh logs, feeding the already raging flames.

The older dancers, with the precision of a close-order drill squad, demonstrate some fancy handiwork with the staves, flicking them straight out then snapping the tips under their arms, whooping and warbling, shaking their trident headdresses in a dramatic tableau as they glide once again around the flaring pyre.

Meanwhile, the women gather quietly in a long swaying line around the outermost circle, trailing one another in a stately procession, a steady, lightsome, soft-shoe shuffle, holding themselves with dignity and ease, hands clasped under the tasseled fringe of their colorful serapes, faces pointed at the sky, lost in thought — proud, strong, indefatigable — giving homage in their own quiet way to the familiar gods that the men are celebrating.

"Women are the lifeblood of the tribe," Harry whispers. "They keep it alive. They keep us alive."

Gleaming rivulets of flame bubble and churn between the blazing logs as a gusty wind ripples across the grass, punching the fire so that it flares in every direction. The wood crew, faces averted or shielded with hooded sweatshirts, haul heavy logs and limbs to the edge of the scalding blaze.

Harry cruises in and out of the family pavilion at a stately pace. He never seems to get rattled or distracted. At one point he appears with a small drum and a stick that he taps tentatively before heading out along the outer rim of the circle to join his singing/drumming compatriots. He has exchanged his ball cap for a stylish straw hat. People notice him as he eases across the grass proscenium. They reach out to shake his hand. He looks like a leader. He acts like one.

In the tipi that afternoon, Eugene told me that all the Indians, not just the Chiricahua Apache, look forward to the Mountain Spirit dances. "It's a celebration," he said. "We have managed to survive another year. We are alive as a people. We will continue to survive and flourish as a people as long as we remain part of the circle."

There's so much going on out here that I know nothing about. The hooting, cooing, clucking of the dancers in imitation of a menagerie of birds. What stories are being told here in the steady, stylish, choreographed movements of the dancers? For example, what does the swaying motion of the dancers signify? The shoulder roll of the lead dancer as he advances toward the fire reminds me of the way the wind swept through the tips of the pine forest deep in the Chiricahua Mountains last winter, igniting the spirits in a twinkling rush.

I am as concerned about this as I am energized. I want it to be true and right and appropriate. I want it to be authentic. I don't want to step somewhere I don't belong. But it feels right. It feels like the way it's supposed to feel. The easy banter with the Mithlo brothers, the careful give and take; perhaps I am more Indian than I think.

I drink a cup of broomweed tea, courtesy of Lavera. "Take four sips," she says, "then open your mouth and breathe deeply. It will help calm your shakes. Drink it down and blow the rest out your mouth."

We sit together, our backs to the dancers and the fire. She tells me, "It's because of what you saw in the Chiricahua last winter. You are a blessed man. Many Apaches go their entire lives without seeing what you saw."

She looks down at the mug. "Four sips of this tea, then open your mouth and breathe deeply."

The taste is dank and tannic. It charges powerfully through my arterial system, inducing a soothing calm. I need to put myself in Melvin's hands. I need to ask him outright to help me. I am afflicted with a couple of nasty maladies — prostate cancer and Parkinson's disease. I need all the help I can get. I feel good — here, now, in this place — with the drums booming and the spirits dancing.

I am here, in this place, with these people. This is where I am supposed to be. It was Harry who said, "We get energy from where we are in the universe. Point, spot, place. This is me. This is where I belong."

How easy that is to say, how difficult to achieve!

Meanwhile, the wood crew throws more limbs and branches into the fire, which crackles loudly between the logs.

Clouds of sparking embers swirl through the air above the fire like a host of blinking insects. I drink more tea. The cool air presses soothingly against my clammy flesh.

There's something dreamlike in the way the dancers drift across the grass, as if suspended in a trance, their bare feet lightly touching the turf — calm, poised, somnambulistic — lost in their motions like mystic sleepwalkers.

The dance ends at midnight, followed by a couple of social dances, boys and girls, face to face, holding hands and shuffling back and forth, stealing quick, giggly kisses.

Six months later, back in Arizona, something happened. Another vision, hallucination, subconscious emanation cast upon the screen of my waking self—this time as I was clambering down the Rhyolite Trail, through the complex layers of frozen magma and granulated tuff that make up the heart of the Chiricahua Mountains. A twisted, anguished, tortured mass of rock, fashioned into spires, figures, hoodoos, columns . . . a massive pile of mysterious statuary, graphically malleable . . . layers and layers of volcanic ash (welded tuff), heaped and piled by eruptive forces some thirty million years ago. As the rocks weathered away, the joints buckled and crashed, widening along zones of obvious weakness . . . a mass of fractures on the verge of collapsing . . . volcanic clouds expanding with hurricane force, avalanching down the slopes before rising into the sky, black, billowy clouds raining down a fine particulate matter as they expand and cool.

I was by myself that day, which wasn't a good idea. The icy trail was ragged and rough, and it would be quite easy to twist an ankle or snap a bone. I had a cell phone, which I left in the car in the visitor center parking lot. Surely if something happened someone would come along and give me a hand.

I've been lucky in situations like that. I've had missteps and sprawled face down or backwards on my ass, but I've never been seriously hurt. I've never taken a header off a cliff or tumbled from a tree. I've never fallen off a horse or been accosted by a bear or a mountain lion.

The time was 9 a.m. I retied the laces on my boots and started down from the top of Sugarloaf Mountain, heading into the coolish edge of a late-winter, high-desert breeze curling up from the conifer depths of the national forest that clung to the base of the mountain complex. After the first few minutes I noticed that my legs no longer felt as plucky as they once did, especially on those stretches where the trail tilted steeply or wrapped itself around a sharp bend. I needed to go slow. Terrain I might have skipped down like a gazelle thirty years ago must be cautiously navigated today. The last thing I wanted was to fall; not many people used this trail, especially in winter.

The route was paved with tessellated slabs of broken stone into a stair-step configuration, with clumps of snow and ice lining the sides as the trail sank deeper into Echo Canyon. The silence was acute. An occasional bird peeped and twittered. I could sense that I was being observed by something — what, I didn't know. (Bigfoot, maybe, sent by Melvin to check on me!) Cranky flies, warmed by the sun, buzzed around my ears. Brassy sentinel flies, on guard in spots gouged and slotted by running water, checking my credentials, wondering who I was and why I was there.

Spanish bayonet bloomed in the interstices between chunks of broken rock, along with prickly pear, cholla, and brush oak. The trail was a jumble of eroded rock faces, carved and buffed by ice and snow into bizarre and fanciful shapes: temples, columns, pillars, hoodoos. Cautiously, like a soldier on point, alert to the possibility of ambush, I made my way onto a narrow ridge that ladled down into an open streambed, marked on the map "Lower Rhyolite Creek." Thousands of years of deposits from side creeks had mounded the bed into a wide, shelf-like table, dotted with major desert flora — palmettos, cottonwoods, oaks, sycamores. Big trees, nourished by side creeks cutting down through the slope of the canyon trail, meshed their canopies into a dense arboreal buffer.

The air was warmer down here at the bottom of the canyon. I had the distinct impression that I was returning to the place where I was born. I heard voices, squeals, the cries of children, horses snorting, the crackle of wood fires along the width of the broad shelf that stretched from the streambed to the ridge line, down through which for the past three hours I had limped and hobbled. Round rocks, tumbled downstream like crude marbles by spring floods, dotted the shelf; bits of wiry understory, the detritus of flowing water, shadowed by a tattered canopy of branches and leaves, a cloudy, ragged ceiling through which the sun slanted in bright, gleaming patches. Ahead of me and to my right I noticed a truncated tree that gradually morphed the more I looked at it into the head and body of a woman. An old woman — ancient and decrepit — standing in the trail, looking at me fixedly as I came toward her.

My pace slowed to a shuffle as I focused on muffling the knock of my boots against the shattered rock. *What's going on here?* I wondered for the umpteenth time that day. I blinked and blinked again. The more I blinked the more familiar the figure became, her body shrouded and featureless as the body of a gah'e. Closer now, the figure of the wraith was unmistakable. Her skin was papery and dry—a wizened crone clad in layers of filthy black weeds.

I stood motionless maybe twenty feet away, close enough to discern a trio of indentations indicating where her eyes and mouth would be if she had such features to display. I sensed that, if I kept walking along the trail to where she stood, the outline of her figure would inevitably morph back into the stolid, featureless stoutness of the truncated tree. I proceeded slowly and gingerly, not wanting to let go of the mirage, curious at the same time as to what would happen.

With her left hand, palm up, she beckoned, brushing the fingers of her right hand across the pink palm, in a beckoning gesture. She didn't confront me face on but rather obliquely, at an angle, as if peering down into something, gesturing with her fingers, urging me not to hesitate, but to come closer.

How long this lasted I have no idea; the more she tapped her palm with the forefinger of her other hand, the more reddish the skin became, as if discolored by a subcutaneous bruise. From this distance I saw her face, the outline of her eyes and mouth, the sheath of her featureless skull. I recognized who she was, but at the same time I did not know who she was or why she should be standing where she was standing. She was clearly from another world, possibly a Little One from the Mountain Spirits pantheon.

I glanced down at my hands, the palms of both hands, but especially my right hand, glowing like a high-voltage lamp.

In a creaky voice she said, "You must make your life easy and smooth."

Who was she? What did she want? Why was she there? Why was I there?

"When you need help, ask for it."

She scratched her fingertips against the palm of her left hand like my grandmother used to do when she was irritated about something. Later, when I tell Harry about the event, I say I think that the image of the woman is a product of both the Parkinson's and the medicine I take every day to contain it. Harry says it's more than that. He insists it's a signal, an omen, a portent.

"The woman is telling you that she has the power to heal you. You need to do what she says," said Harry. "It's time you behaved like an Apache."

It was then that I realized that Apache medicine was so powerful it was solution-driven; not just diagnostic, but deeply curative. "Do you want a long life?" the crone whispered. 'You must make your mind smooth. No kinks or knots. Ussen says for you to be watchful. He says your worst enemy is yourself. You must detect danger before it detects you."

How long I was held in thrall by this vision I cannot say. Then, sure enough, as I continued down the path toward the visitor center, the figure behind me, twisted and gnarly, spooky and dark, melted away into the morning air.

WATSON

I had no formal education, but I could read and write. I taught myself to read the newspaper by copying words down from the comic strips. The words were simple and easy to understand.

In 1929 the United States suffered a serious economic depression. Suddenly, nobody had anything, certainly not the Indians who never had anything to begin with. I needed to earn money to help feed my family. Recycling seemed a good way for a man to earn a little money at a time when money was scarce for everyone. So I walked the roads around Fort Sill collecting scrap iron, soda bottles, milk bottles, which I sold back to the grocery store for cash.

In 1935 I joined the Civilian Conservation Corps (CCC) and got my training at Fort Cobb, Oklahoma, along with a number of other young Indian men. Our schooling took place in the Indian Baptist Church, located east of Fort Cobb. The instructors taught us how to measure lumber with a folding ruler, how to cut lumber with a handsaw and a two-man saw, how to use a hammer and nails, how to mix and pour concrete, and, most important, how to work together as a team.

Throughout Oklahoma there were many CCC camps. Among the men with me at Fort Cobb were Bud Wells, Dixon Palmer, Floyd Paddyaker, and Harry Guy. We earned twenty-one dollars a month. We had three meals a day, hot and cold running water, a warm bed to sleep in at night. The camp gave us proper instruction for making a living and learning how to work for ourselves. Harry Guy and the others learned how to landscape and plant rows of windbreak trees, which they later used to good effect in the towns of Stecker, Apache, Fort Cobb, and Carnegie. They also planted scores of fruit trees.

The CCC camp we were assigned to was located west of the town of Apache on the Albert Attocknie allotment. George Asepermy, a Comanche, was the camp boss. One day we were working on a project in the hot sun when we broke for lunch. A man named Clarence Sankadota lay down in the shade of a cottonwood tree and rolled around in the dust like a dog until he was completely comfortable. A few minutes later the camp boss said, "Okay, the break is over. Let's get back to work."

Clarence stared at George Asepermy. "Boss," he said. "I can't work anymore. I'm dog-tired."

The name stuck. Thereafter, Clarence was called "Dog-tired."

Old Man Gooday had many Mountain Spirit dances at his home, northwest of Apache. The Mescalero Apache people came regularly from New Mexico to feast and dance and renew their Oklahoma friendships. Sometimes we called the Mountain Spirit Dance the Horn Dance because of the elaborate crowns the dancers wear. Sometimes the dance lasted two days, sometimes four—usually four, because that's a sacred number for the Apache.

In 1940, Old Man Gooday and his wife Bessie planned a trip to Mescalero. They offered a ride to my aunt Tsis-tohn and my niece Doris, both of whom lived in Mescalero. After enjoying a long stay with us at Fort Sill, they were ready to go home.

Back in 1940, a trip by automobile to New Mexico took about eighteen hours. Old Man Gooday drove and Bessie sat in the front seat next to him. The car was what was called a touring car, with a retractable roof that could be installed in a jiffy to keep the sun out of the faces of the people inside.

Shortly after they got underway, Bessie and Old Man Gooday began drinking. This went on for miles, until they started shouting at each other. Old Man Gooday finally stopped the car and they continued to fuss and bicker by the side of the road, circling the parked vehicle like a pair of coyotes, first in one direction, then the other. After a while, they fell silent and got back in the car. Old Man Gooday started the car. The engine fired up and the car rumbled down the road.

"Well, I'm glad we got that straightened out," Gooday said. "Now we can go to Mescalero."

My niece Doris was just a young girl, but she clearly remembers the altercation. Aunt Tsis-tohn slept through the whole thing.

In 1914, we read in the newspapers that Germany had declared war on Great Britain and France. In 1917, when the United States entered the war, I went to sign up at Fort Sill. This was my chance to join the U.S. Army and see the world! They checked my arms, hands, feet, legs, knees, and head. They told me that they couldn't accept me because of my eye injury.

I explained to them how I had received the injury. The sergeant said, "Well, Chief, I think you've been fighting for too long already. You Apache guys are tough customers. I'm sorry, but the Army can't accept you if you have only one eye."

I went back home to Apache, fuming inside. I couldn't tolerate anyone calling me "Chief." I wasn't a chief. White people have no respect when they call an Indian "Chief." My name was Watson Mithlo. The term "Chief" used this way was a racist slur. I had never called a white person "White Boy," because I felt it was disrespectful to call someone by a name other than his or her own.

One night in September 1939 we heard on the radio that the German Army had invaded Poland. Another war in Europe had begun. Maybe this war they would let me enlist and serve overseas. But I was too old and got turned down again.

People think Indians are patriotic, and they are, but it's more complicated than that. America is our country too. We were here first; we have always been here, and we always will be. We defended ourselves and our land against the U.S. Army and did a pretty good job of it for 400 years. If the Germans and Japanese wanted to conquer America, they would have to go through its native people to get the job done, and we weren't about to let that happen. We knew a lot about fighting. We were good at it. We were Apaches.

One evening after dinner at the CCC headquarters, Bud, Dixon, Floyd, and Harry Guy sat around, smoking and discussing the best way to make money. Someone mentioned the United States Army National Guard. In 1939, fifteen American Indians went to Anadarko and joined the National Guard.

In the aftermath of the Pearl Harbor attack, the 45th (Oklahoma) National Guard division was federalized and made a part of the regular army. Eventually the entire 45th Division went to Fort Sill to learn how to operate field artillery. They soon became an elite unit; their knowledge of the big guns, especially the 155 mm howitzer, enabled them to train new recruits.

In 1940, my brother Harry was sent to Camp Barclay, southwest of Abilene, Texas. General George S. Patton was there with his First Cavalry — real horse cavalry, with tooting horns and brass buttons and gleaming saddlery, the spit and polish for which George Patton was famous. The Indians in the unit performed tribal dances while they were at the camp, much to General Patton's delight. They did not have the proper regalia to do tribal dancing, but they danced in their boots and made do with what they had.

Harry Mithlo was at Camp Barclay with the 45th Division when the Japanese attacked Pearl Harbor on December 7, 1941. Melvin Longhorn, Dixon Palmer, and Floyd Paddyaker were home on leave from Camp Barclay. They were standing on top of Mount Scott in the Wichita Mountains Wildlife Refuge, near Fort Sill, when they heard about the attack.

Mount Scott is the tallest mountain in the Wichita system, located north and west of Fort Sill. It's possible that Geronimo was reburied that frosty February night in 1909 somewhere close by. The Kiowa Indians believe that all the buffalo left in the world live inside Mount Scott, waiting for the moment when they can be released to walk the earth again, free and unfettered.

The men thought about running away, all the way to California if necessary, and getting on a boat and sailing to a safe, secluded corner of the world, where they could live their lives like they wanted. But there wasn't any safe, secluded spot left on earth, and there hadn't been since they left the Chiricahua Mountains in the Arizona Territory in 1886 and were herded onto the trains at Holbrook and sent to Florida as prisoners of war.

The three men talked and prayed and smoked. Then they came down off the mountain and reported for duty at the National Guard headquarters in Anadarko, Oklahoma.

It's no dishonor for an Apache to wear the uniform of a soldier in the U.S Army. We fought them long and hard, and we have nothing to be ashamed of. Even the anthropologists agree the Apache were the most cunning and capable of the native enemies the Army faced. I volunteered for service, but they wouldn't take me. I seethed and snarled, then gradually came to accept it. Two eyes in combat are better than one. I remember hearing stories from my mother about warriors who could pluck out their eyes and toss them high up into a tree, where they could see the enemy and know exactly where he was and what he was doing.

My brother Harry Mithlo completed his training in Boston, Massachusetts, then went on for more training at Camp Pickett in the Blue Ridge Mountains of Virginia. Before being shipped overseas, Harry and his friends had a three-day pass to New York City. They had heard about Jack Dempsey's famous bar and restaurant in midtown Manhattan. They met Jack, the former heavyweight boxing champion of the world. Born and raised in rural Colorado, Jack understood Indians. He took good care of Harry and his friends. He paid for their food and drinks. He took pride in being able to honor American Indian soldiers from Oklahoma.

In 1943, the 45th Division sailed safely across the U-boat-infested North Atlantic Ocean to North Africa, where they deployed for action. Harry and his comrades participated in the invasion of Sicily in July 1943. There wasn't much fighting when the division first landed near the city of Caserta on the southern coast. Soon there was lots of action, though, with the Germans pulling back to the foothills which they could defend better with their deadly 88 mm guns. Harry's unit got into the thick of it; on high ground with their self-propelled 105 mm howitzer, they were directed by an officer to take out a German machine gun nest lodged in a concrete bunker that was holding up their attack. It took Harry several rounds, but the bunker was destroyed.

Harry thereafter transferred to George Patton's Third Army. He was a good soldier and he knew it, but the officers in the Oklahoma National Guard Division retained a lingering prejudice against Indian soldiers serving in the ranks. Patton didn't care where you were from as long as you wanted to fight. Harry was ambitious, a natural soldier, and he wanted to fight.

In September 1943, Harry was part of the invasion force that landed at Salerno, on the Italian peninsula. Fighting was heavy; opposing the American invasion at this point were several crack German panzer divisions.

During the battle, Dixon Palmer guided the men to a tomb in the depths of a cemetery that came under intense shelling. Floyd Paddyaker didn't like being in the cemetery with all the dead bodies, but Palmer reassured him that the dead couldn't harm them: "They're already dead!"

The men hunkered down in the cemetery until the shelling stopped. Dixon Palmer insisted that the Germans never shelled anything with a graveyard in it. "As long as we stay here," he said, "we'll be okay."

When the shelling stopped, the men made their way back to their unit.

Several months later, during the worst of the battle at Monte Cassino southeast of Rome, Floyd Paddyaker was a forward observer for his battery unit. Harry Mithlo, promoted to staff sergeant, was in charge of two half-track vehicles that carried ammunition to the soldiers on the firing line.

One day a message from headquarters told Harry to pull back his units. Harry and his half-track driver drove to the firing line to make sure that all the units had pulled back. Harry's driver radioed that they were at the firing line, waiting for the last vehicle to pull back.

A few minutes later a call came in: "Sergeant Mithlo doesn't answer!"

Headquarters called the code numbers again for Sergeant Mithlo. The air crackled with dry static. There was still no answer. Finally a voice said, "Sergeant Mithlo's vehicle took a direct hit."

After a brief silence, the voice said, "Does anyone know Sergeant Mithlo?"

Floyd Paddyaker knew Harry but he did not respond. He didn't want to see Harry dead, covered with blood. He didn't want to remember him that way.

Harry was killed during some of the worst fighting at Monte Cassino. The weather was cold, the ground covered with snow. Repeated bombings by American and British aircraft had reduced the beautiful monastery to a heap of blasted stone and rubble.

Harry was a warrior to the bone. There's no denying that. He had the instincts of a born fighter. As a kid he liked to listen to the old people tell stories of their battles with the Mexicans and the Blue Coats.

When he was a teenager, he was taught the rudiments of combat by these same elders. They knew how duck and bob and weave. They knew how to crawl on their bellies, showing no more profile than a snake.

I'll never forget the day his parents, Lawrence and Dolly Mithlo, received a telegram from the War Department informing them of Harry's death. It was a sad day. The sky was filled with gloomy clouds. We built a fire and beat a drum and prayed to Ussen.

In 1943, just before Harry was killed, I worked at Fort Sill driving a truck for the sanitation service. I was given two helpers on my truck route, two German soldiers, in their early twenties, who had been taken prisoner in North Africa. They had fought for Field Marshal Erwin Rommel. They were good workers and were eager to help out in any way they could.

We spent a lot of time together. They asked lots of questions about the Apache Indians. They were curious as to where the Apache people came from and how they ended up where they did. I told them the story of our people, how they were removed from Arizona and shipped like cattle in railroad cars to St. Augustine, Florida. I told them about life in the Mount Vernon Barracks in Alabama, and the journey out to Fort Sill in the Oklahoma Territory. They were interested to learn that I was also a former prisoner of war of the United States Army. We had that in common. The difference was that we Apache were prisoners for twenty-seven years, the Germans for two.

The Germans became good friends. They never got enough to eat in their mess halls, so I took them to eat in mine. I knew all the cooks in the mess halls, and I had no trouble getting them something to eat. I also brought them candy and cigarettes.

I lost my two helpers in May 1945, when the war ended. Later that year, all German prisoners were removed from Fort Sill and sent back to Europe.

Two of my sons, Harry and Eugene, served in the military during the Vietnam War. One day Harry, who was born in 1944, told his mom and me that he had joined the Navy. Two years later, after completing his Navy stint, he joined the Army. He served on a destroyer escort as a sailor and was with the Adjutant General Corps in the Army.

Eugene was born in 1946 and served as a combat infantryman in the 9th Infantry Division in Vietnam.

My wife Lavina and I cried when they left to go overseas. We sat together under the trees on the north side of the house and held hands and prayed that all the boys from Apache would come home safely.

Harry was in the U.S. Army in 1964, stationed in New Jersey. Vietnam was about ready to explode. When news arrived that his wife was about to have a baby, he was told to go home to Lawton to be with her.

One cool foggy morning in November, he started out for home. He had ten dollars in his pocket, so he hitchhiked most of the way and walked the rest. He was in uniform and carried a B4 bag with his clothes and belongings. I can see him now, pausing near a ramp on the New Jersey turnpike, a solid, self-contained man, shuffling westward, plodding on course, determined to make it home before the baby (his first child) was born.

"I got rides easy," he told me later. "It was the uniform and the color of my skin. When I told them I was an Apache Indian from Chihuahua's band, they were very respectful."

He added, "It was before the Vietnam War turned sour in everyone's mouth."

He spent a night or two out in the open, in a field or pasture, eating food he had purchased in a grocery store. "Walking is the way to go, feeling your feet strike the earth, with the energy and resonance of a drum. If they didn't pick me up, they at least saluted as they sped by. You get into a mood and you can go all day and night. I was like a big honey bear clumping across the landscape, looking for a bee hive. It's amazing the power that the surface of the earth carries. The more I walked, the better I felt."

I have been fighting a long time: from the time my mother carried me in her womb in 1886; from the time the Apache people were forced into exile in Florida and Alabama in the late 1880s; from the time we were transferred to new quarters at Fort Sill in 1894; from the time my oldest son Roy served in World War II as a U.S. Navy Air Cadet; from the time my brother Harry died in Italy in 1943. I may not actually have carried a rifle or worn a helmet, but vicariously through the bravery of my brothers and sons and nephews, I have served my country in its time of need.

After the Second World War, I took any job that came my way. For a while I drove a truck for the Apache Flour Company, which was owned by a German man whom I respectfully called Old Man Peeper. I delivered Falcon Flour to the surrounding towns. If I couldn't make the run in one day, I'd sleep in the truck. The short runs I made easily in one day. On those days I'd return before closing and help sack the flour for the next day's run. Two other men worked at milling the flour: Sam Tahmahkera and John Flute. They helped unload the wheat farmers' trucks. We worked fourteen – to sixteen-hour days, especially during the May and June harvests. Next came the tractors and the plowing of the fields to prepare for the replanting of the wheat before the autumn rains began. It was hard work, but it was steady and satisfying.

Old Man Peeper's son Herman owned a hardware store next door to the flour company. My son Harry used to plow for him. Harry began working as a teenager during summer vacations. He was a big, broad-shouldered kid even as a teenager, and he did a lot of heavy lifting for the local people, Indians and white.

My friend Sam Tahmahkera was a descendant of Comanche chief Quanah Parker. Sam was married to a Comanche woman named Eva Tate; they lived five miles east of the village of Apache on the road to Cyril. Sam and Eva had a son named Carl Tahmahkera. I went to see Sam when he became sick and was taken to the Lawton hospital. He was glad to see me and shook my hand; a few days later, he died.

John Flute was a hard-working Indian who lived alone; my sister Garnett Mithlo was his girlfriend. John worked hard in the flour mill. He milled the flour, sacked it in different weight-cloth sacks, and sewed the stops shut. He always helped me load the flour truck for the next day's delivery.

I liked driving around the countryside, even though I'd been on the same road a hundred times before. I never tired of it; I always felt replenished at the end of the day when I drove the truck home. I was never alone. I never felt abandoned. The spirits were with me every step of the way. The ancestors. The people.

One day a white man from Fort Sill came to speak to me. He said he came from the Fort Sill Museum. His name was Gillett Griswold, formerly with the Historical Section of the U.S. Army in Europe during World War II.

In 1954, he came to Fort Sill to be director of the museum. Under his leadership, the museum became the U.S. Army's largest military and historical museum. Mr. Griswold told me he was interested in the Apache prisoners of war who were held at Fort Sill before they were released in 1914. Of particular interest to him were the photos and names of the prisoners.

I had several old photographs that he asked to copy. He said he would return them as soon as possible. He found one photo to be especially compelling, that of an Apache prisoners of war group in which the men were standing or sitting on the porch of the Apache prisoners of war office. The people in the photo included Jason Betzinez, Walter Louie, Richard Imach, Johnny Loco, James Kawaykla, and some other prisoners, including myself. I told him I was reluctant to hand over the pictures to someone other than an Apache. But Mr. Griswold was very persuasive. He promised to make copies for himself and return the originals to me.

Three weeks went by and my pictures were not returned. I went to the Fort Sill Museum to see Mr. Griswold. He said he was glad to see me. I asked him to give me back my original photographs. He disappeared into a storage area and came back empty-handed. "I can't find it," he said. "But I know it's back there somewhere."

I never got that photograph back from the Fort Sill Museum. It's another sad story of culture theft. I know many Indian people who had important historical and cultural items — weapons, cradleboards, clothes, ceremonial articles — taken from them by well-meaning White Eyes. Did they think we didn't care? Did they think we didn't know what was important to us and what wasn't? These things belong to the Chiricahua Apache and nobody else.

One bright summer day my sons Harry and Eugene were working with me in my backyard in Apache, Oklahoma, when we spotted an airplane overhead, traveling north. The airplane was flying fast, trailing a plume of white smoke. We watched until it faded out of sight. Minutes later, we saw the airplane coming back from the north, traveling fast. The white smoke pouring out the tail turned black then red as flames erupted around the wings. We watched helplessly as the airplane blew apart and fell in fiery pieces to the ground.

Later I learned that the airplane was called a B-58 Hustler. It took a while for the military to collect all the mechanical parts strewn about from the explosion; it took even longer to account for the remains of the crew.

Some people are convinced that the story about the crash of the B-58 Hustler is really a story about the Mountain Spirits, or the Little People as they are called. Few people have actually seen them. The warrior Juh saw them one time on the high flat mountain where he lived, the same place where Eugene Chihuahua saw them. "It was up on that high flat mountain where the warrior Juh lived where I saw the Little People," Eugene said. "I thought at first that it was a child about four or five years old and that it might be separated from its mother, but when I got close I saw that he was a grown man. I told nobody but Asa Daklugie, who explained the phenomenon to me. 'There are Little People living in the forest,' Asa said, 'and they sometimes come around the outskirts of a village. They are not ghosts or witches; they are small people with horns sticking out of their heads. They are here to help us, and they never die."

CONGER

Ask an Apache about what took place at Roswell, New Mexico, in 1947 and he will have an answer. He might not share it with you, but then he doesn't want you to think that whatever reply he makes is too far-fetched or fantastical. If he does respond, he is simply reporting what he regards as fact. He knows what that incident was about: Some white people think the military took several dead aliens out of the wreckage of a flying saucer, but they didn't; the creatures inside the ship were Little People, on their way to help the Apache. Melvin told me that the Little People appear when the Chiricahua need them for something, and they remain there until the problem is solved. They're diminutive, but very powerful. Physically, they are the antithesis of the heroes of the White Eyes culture, which extols people of big physical size. John Wayne types, Viking-types, Paul Bunyan types, truck-driver types, pro football offensive tackle types. By contrast, the "Little People" are just that: little in size, but gifted with the ability to help and heal those who need helping and healing.

I marked the place where the B-58 Hustler came out of the sky in a burst of flame and fell to the ground. The Little People had something to do with this. I'm just sure of it.

WATSON

In February 1963, our son Kenneth Chasenah was in a car wreck on Indian Road, a mile and a half from Fort Cobb. He lost control of the wheel and the car plunged off the road and down the bank of a tributary of Washita Creek. The car was found by Dennis Horsechief, the son of Donald and Mary Horsechief. Dennis went down into the creek to play on the ice. As he walked toward the cement bridge that crossed the creek, he spotted a car with a person hanging out the door, his legs in the water. Dennis ran back home to tell his father. Donald Horsechief arrived at the scene to find that the crash victim had pulled his jacket over his head in an attempt to warm himself. Donald and his wife Mary covered the victim with blankets and built a fire. A neighbor called an ambulance and the State Highway Patrol.

When Kenneth failed to come home on Saturday night, Lavina and I went looking for him. We were notified that he had been in a car wreck and was on his way to the hospital. Kenneth lost both legs, as well as several fingers, to frostbite. His uncle, Eugene Chihuahua, said he survived because he was a Mountain Spirit dancer and the spirits wouldn't let him die.

Are we chronically marked for failure because we are Indians? It wasn't this way in the old days; at least it wasn't as bad. Being Indian is to agree to let everything happen that is supposed to happen, according to the cosmic ebb and flow. People, both whites and Indians, died in droves fighting other folks whom they regarded as patently inferior. We never have been able to shed this reputation; we carry it with us wherever we go. If we had banded together on the Atlantic seaboard when the pilgrims first waded ashore and presented a united front, we would still hold this land as our own. Instead, we compromised, we relaxed our guard, we let the White Eyes take what they wanted. And they wanted all of it.

I have been fortunate to see many new things in my life. I remember the time I saw my first candy bar and my first pack of cigarettes (as opposed to each one being hand rolled). I remember the first time I heard news being broadcast on the radio. The telephone was an equally amazing invention. All of these were wonderful, but my favorite was television. I saw a show from New York featuring actual people dancing and singing on a stage. I heard and saw rockets going into outer space. I watched a man in a bulky white suit walk on the surface of the moon.

For some reason that didn't sit right with me. I thought it was wrong. If there's nothing up there, why go there? That kind of information belongs exclusively to Ussen. Only He can understand what that means.

In 1960, Benedict Jozhe Jr. and I flew to Washington, DC, to locate the gravesite of Taza, the son of Chief Cochise, who died of pneumonia while on a good-will trip to Washington in 1876. Back then, a man named John Clum was superintendent of the Chiricahua Reservation, which then was located on the San Carlos Reservation in central Arizona. John Clum thought that everything on the reservation was peaceful enough for him to mix a little pleasure with business, so he boarded a train and rode to Ohio and got married. Taza went on to Washington, where he contracted pneumonia and died. His brother Naiche became the Chiricahua leader, but he was less gifted a leader even than Taza had been. The Chiricahuas found the circumstances of Taza's death mysterious; they suspected witchcraft. Naiche could only look on helplessly as the once powerful Chiricahua split into factions.

With the help of the U.S. Park Service, Benedict Jozhe and I were able to locate the gravesite. All the Apache people knew was that Taza went to Washington, DC, where he died, and that his body was never returned. The Fort Sill Apache Business Committee had requested that Benedict Jozhe and I travel to the capital and locate his grave in order to place a granite marker at the site.

Benedict Jozhe was an Apache prisoner of war, born in captivity at Fort Sill in April 1908. He married a Comanche woman named Rachel Martinez, and they had two daughters. Benedict served as the chairman of the Business Committee for the Fort Sill Apaches before they achieved tribal status.

Years later, Benedict and I worked together again, this time with Moses Loco, to locate the sites of the original twelve Chiricahua Apache villages at Fort Sill.

My trip with Benedict to Washington in 1960 marked the first time I had ever flown in an airplane. I had walked, ridden a horse, ridden on a wagon, sat in a train, sat in an automobile, sat in a boat, rode a bicycle, clung to the leather strap of a streetcar, and now flown in an airplane! It was a lot like riding in an automobile only with the windows tightly rolled up. It was disappointing in one respect: Because of the height at which we flew, it was difficult to make out the features on the ground.

Was I seeing something from the same perspective as a mountain spirit? I couldn't answer that. Possibly so. I was a dancer. I knew what it was like to be transported in the clutch of the spirits from one point in the landscape to another. That was the easy part. Teleportation was one thing, spirit flight another. You had to understand the practical side of the situation before the big thing actually took place. And when it did you had to be discreet and say nothing to anyone. If you talked too much about it, you got branded as a witch, men as well as women.

The country was changing. But before it did, I wanted my sons Harry and Eugene to ride in a steam-powered locomotive before it was replaced by a diesel locomotive. In 1955 the two boys rode the train from Apache to Anadarko. In 1975, I bought plane tickets for my grandchildren, Lisa and Michael, to fly from Lawton to Oklahoma City. I had enjoyed my first airplane ride back in 1960 so much that I wanted my children and grandchildren to have the same experience.

While prisoners at Fort Sill, the Apaches lived in twelve villages or settlements. The villages were named in honor of chiefs, warriors, and important people: Naiche, Chatto, Loco, Mangus, Toclanny, Kay-ahtennay, Noche, Chihuahua, Geronimo, Kayiah, Perico, and Chiricahua Tom.

In 1970, Moses Loco, Benedict Johze, and I located these former villages on the Fort Sill grounds. The soldiers helped us with their bayonets and mine detectors. We found artifacts at each site, which helped us establish their identity and location.

Naiche's village was the main Apache meeting place. Four Mile Crossing near Naiche's camp was the favorite gathering place for gamblers, traders, and whiskey peddlers. All the local tribes came to Four Mile Crossing to dance, gamble, and palaver. It was located across Medicine Creek, four miles west of the Fort Sill Headquarters.

When she was in the eighth grade, my granddaughter Lisa Mithlo was shot in the back while she was a student at the Apache Elementary school. The children were playing in the schoolyard when the principal walked up to her and pointed a pistol at her back and pulled the trigger. The pistol fired blanks, but it left serious burn marks on her skin.

What was the man thinking? Lisa recovered, but the incident scarred her for life. For someone to point a gun at someone else is tantamount to "killing" that person.

The school board did not reprimand the principal. Why would anyone, especially a professional educator, do something like that?

It made no sense. It was thoughtless and cruel.

My grandson Michael often stayed with my wife Lavina and me at our house in Apache. He was a good boy, a smart boy. I used to tell him to "look into the eyes of a buffalo, and you will see the universe. They are free like the Apache people."

Sometimes when the weather was hot the three of us would sleep together on a wooden bed in the white shed behind our home. The dirt floor was cool, but Michael's grandmother would fuss at him when she caught him dragging his feet and stirring up the dust. Sometimes at night we were awakened by rainstorms rumbling in the distance. That was the best time to sleep, with warm drops pattering against the grass and trees.

My aunt Tsis-tohn got the surprise of her life one day in the 1940s when she stepped inside an elevator in a department store in downtown Lawton, Oklahoma. The door closed and the room started to make noises. The walls shook and groaned; when the door opened, she was in a different place. The room had transported her from the bottom floor to the sixth floor, and she didn't have to lift a foot to get there!

Tsis-tohn didn't speak English very well. One time she traveled alone round-trip by bus from Oklahoma to New Mexico, on to Arizona, then back to Apache, Oklahoma. We couldn't figure out how she did it; she must have used sign language or had someone write notes for her.

She was shrewd about money. She was from the old school; she liked to bargain the price of an item down as low as she could get it. She took her niece Alvina along with her when she shopped. Alvina spoke Apache, and Tsis-tohn was always urging her to cut a dollar or two off the price. Alvina was from the new school, where bartering was considered rude and ill-mannered. Alvina didn't like being in the middle of a heated exchange. Aunt Tsis-tohn would tell Alvina that she wished she herself had gone to the white man's school so she could speak English for herself. She could really get into a good argument then.

In 1990, I was asked by the American Indian Student Association at the University of Oklahoma in Norman to attend an honoring ceremony for Allan Houser and Rigoberta Menchú. Allan Houser was the son of Sam Houser, a former Fort Sill Apache prisoner of war. Allan was a fine artist and sculptor. Many of his works are on display in museums and galleries all over the country. I was asked to sing Chiricahua Apache songs, which he enjoyed. Rigoberta Menchú is a gentle, dedicated Indian woman from Guatemala, awarded the Nobel Peace Prize in 1992 for her international promotion of Indigenous peoples' rights. I was deeply honored to meet such a special Indian lady.

Indian people are the same everywhere. We all face the same problems. We all struggle against the same enemies.

The evening started out with thunder and rain, a good sign. The rain stopped, and we could smell the wet grass and leaves. That night in Norman was terribly exciting. My sons and grandsons were with me and we sang Round Dance songs and Back and Forth Apache songs that got the people out on the floor, dancing. We sang at the University Field House, north of the football stadium. The room was packed with students and members from about every tribe in North America. Allan Houser danced and so did Rigoberta Menchú. It was a memorable night, and we all had a good time.

In 1981, Charles Banks Wilson came to my home in Apache to paint a portrait of me. He was illustrating a new book on full-blood American Indians, and he traveled all over the country to find them. At first I didn't trust him and didn't know if I should cooperate on the project. He came to my house equipped with lamps, paper, and pencils. I sat for the portrait, and he talked about the importance of the project. There weren't many full-bloods left anywhere in the nation, and he was determined to capture the features and expressions of those who were still alive. I told him the story of how the Chiricahua people came to Oklahoma.

In 1983, an exhibition of full-blood Indian portraits by Charles Banks Wilson was held at the Blue Room in the State Capitol Building in Oklahoma City. My portrait was featured along with many others. I hadn't known that Wilson was such a famous artist. He seemed really pleased that so many Indian people attended the reception for the publication of the new book, which was titled *Search for the Purebloods.*

Each day I walked the boundary line around the property of our home in Apache, checking the fences just like I used to do when I was a prisoner of war at Fort Sill. The fence was continuous from the house up to the north boundary, all the way east to Cache Creek. The creekbank fence then ran a half-mile to the south, before returning to the house. Weather permitting, I walked this fence line every day.

One day as I was walking along the creek bank, I heard someone whistling. Then, a few moments later, I was jolted by a blast of wind. Someone wanted me for something. Whoever was whistling wanted to catch my attention. I walked out of the creek bottom and turned back toward the creek to see who had whistled. But as I turned my face to look, I saw no one. I didn't know what to think, so I continued on my walk.

When I got to the house Lavina looked at me. "What's wrong with your mouth?"

My face felt numb, as if something was trying to tear it off the bone and drag it down to the ground.

"Your mouth is turned downward," she said.

I tried to drink water but the water trickled out the side of my mouth. I realized that I was unable to talk.

"We're going to see Chief," she said.

Oliver Pahdopony was respectfully called "Chief." He lived out on the prairie several miles east of Apache. He was the last of the traditional Comanche medicine men, and his medicine ways were well-known throughout Indian country. Chief learned the medicine for "twisted face" from a healer named Comanche Jack. It was said that Comanche Jack's medicine was so strong it took only one visit to deliver a satisfactory cure.

We drove fast to Chief's house. When we arrived, Lavina lit a cigarette and handed it to Chief, the customary way to ask for help from traditional medicine people. Chief asked what we wanted, and after we explained what had happened, he doctored me four times and afterwards my mouth was completely healed and there was no sign that I had been afflicted with anything. I was cured in a traditional spiritual way, and I never had the problem again.

It is not within Comanche culture to declare oneself a "medicine man." Others might refer to someone as a medicine man, but Comanches never refer to themselves in that way. My son Melvin acquired some of his healing ability from Chief. Chief took Melvin aside one day and told him about the medicine; he handed down the medicine ways to Melvin. In this traditional fashion, Chief's medicine lives on.

Creeks, streams, and rivers are full of spirits, some good, some bad. When they were very young, I warned my children not to linger along a watercourse before it gets dark because the spirits might do bad things to you. At the same time, they did good things. It all depends on their mood. If they want to help you, they will.

Life is a constant challenge for us Indians. The deeper we delve into the spirit world, the more responses we stir up. The spirits can be helpful or they can make your life a living hell. I always tried to do the correct thing in my dealings with them. I never tried to fool them or shortchange them. When they told me what they wanted I did my best to oblige. I believe they are here to help us.

I've had many problems in my life, but I tried not to let them get me down. I always knew what I was doing with my money and my time. Nonetheless, I've been cheated out of a few dollars. The Fort Sill Apache Tribe and the Bureau of Indian Affairs once cheated me out of a lot of money. Here's that story.

In 1949, the Chiricahua Apache prisoners of war filed a claim against the United States Government. We won the claim for the taking of our land and the taking of our natural resources. The prisoners of war claim for wrongful imprisonment was dismissed by the court.

I, along with my children, was paid for the land claim, but I was not paid for the natural resources. The Fort Sill Apaches kept this payment a secret. No one spoke a word to anyone about this claim.

My son Harry later became a high school teacher at the Riverside (Anadarko) Indian Boarding School, one of the oldest Indian boarding schools in the nation. Mr. Bob Gooday was also employed by the school during the time that Harry taught there.

One day Harry was on his way home from school when he stopped by our house to talk about the natural resources payment. He told us that Bob Gooday had told him that in May 1985 the tribe was paid $5,300 per person. Bob asked what Harry had bought with his share of the money. If this conversation had not occurred, neither Harry nor I would ever have known about the natural resources payment.

Harry visited the Fort Sill Apaches and checked on my share of the money. Chairwoman Mildred Cleghorn told him to check with the Bureau of Indian Affairs at the Anadarko (Oklahoma) Agency. The agency said they had mailed out all the checks. I checked with the banks that I had business with in case there might be a sizeable deposit where I had an account. My wife Lavina went to the agency to check on my share of the money. An employee named Irene Lane told her that she may have cashed the check and spent the money and forgot about it.

How could anyone forget the money once they had cashed the check, especially a check that big?

Harry told me that each native person has an individual Indian Monies Statement of Account at the agency. This statement of account shows the date, document date, reference number, check number, and amount taken from the account and the balance. Lavina went to see Arnold Tate at the agency to get the statement of account for the year 1985. Inexplicably, Mr. Tate had copies of all the monthly statements except for the month of May 1985. According to Mr. Tate, that particular statement was missing. "I cannot find the month of May 1985," he confessed.

Why would a monthly account be missing unless someone removed or destroyed the month's account? I feel that I was robbed of my payment, and that the Fort Sill Apache Tribe never shared the information of the payment with me.

We asked Ronnie Stallings, our mailman for the last twelve years, about the check. He said he did not remember any check for me from the Anadarko Agency. He knew when our retirement checks came each month. When the monthly checks came in he would bring them up to the house rather than leave them in the mailbox on the road where they might be stolen.

There were other incidents with the Fort Sill Apache Tribe. The tribal membership voted to give a special payment to all the tribal elders. I looked forward to this payment, but when I went to the Fort Sill Tribal office to check on it, they turned me away. A person in the office told me, "We're out of money."

How could a tribe be out of money when there are only a handful of elders in the tribe?

My son Harry wrote a letter to Senator David Boren about the check for $5,300 that I never received. In turn, Harry got a sheet of paper with a handwritten note from the Anadarko Agency stating, "The checks were mailed." There was no signature on the note, only someone's initials. There was no further explanation, so we let it go.

I don't know what to say about all this. The Bureau of Indian Affairs simply does not look after the best interests of the Indian people. They certainly do look out for each other and their own interests. The BIA must have needed the $5,300 more than I did.

In 1990, a young man named Lloyd Larkin called me and invited me to be a special guest during the reunion of the 509th Parachute Infantry Battalion World War II Veterans, in Tulsa, Oklahoma. He wanted to talk about the Apache prisoners of war and the life of the warrior Geronimo.

Lloyd Larkin was a member of the 509th Parachute Infantry Battalion during World War II. The men of the 509th were the most decorated parachute battalion in the U.S. Army. Their battle cry was "Geronimo!", which they shouted as they jumped from their airplanes.

Veterans from the 509th came to the reunion from all over the country. Because I was a former prisoner of war at Fort Sill with Geronimo and the others, they made me an honorary member of the unit. I was given a plaque, a unit patch, and a membership certificate. My sons Harry and Melvin, my grandson Michael, and I sang Apache songs to show our appreciation for being asked to participate in the reunion. I was deeply grateful to Lloyd Larkin for including me.

I told Lloyd Larkin that the Apache prisoners of war were forcibly removed from Arizona to Florida in 1886, and that Geronimo was not the last Apache leader to give up his arms. The last Apache leader to give up his arms was Mangus in December 1886. Mangus was the son of Mangas Coloradas, who was tricked into surrendering by the Blue Coats in 1863. After he was killed for "trying to escape," he was beheaded and his skull boiled in a vat of water until the skin peeled off.

I told Lloyd Larkin that, contrary to popular opinion, Geronimo did not surrender to the Blue Coats but rather lay down his arms so he could be with his family and friends. The Blue Coat generals (specifically

General Nelson A. Miles) promised the Chiricahua that if they lay down their arms they would be sent to a place in Florida where they would be with their people. Instead, the warriors were incarcerated at Fort Pickens outside Pensacola, three hundred miles away from the Castillo de San Marcos in Saint Augustine, Florida, where the women and children were quarantined.

WATSON

I knew Chief Nana. I knew Chief Loco and Chief Mangas Coloradas. I knew Chief Chatto, Chief Chihuahua, and Chief Naiche when we were all being held as prisoners of war. Chief Chatto had a keen sense of humor.

Indian people are not the stone-faced gargoyles the White Eyes think we are. We like to tease and laugh at each other and make fun of ourselves. It has always helped us ride over the hump of bad times when we've been able to laugh.

I knew Chief Cochise, I knew Chief Victorio, I knew Chief Juh, I knew the legendary Woman Warrior, Lozen.

All the Apache men of my day served as warriors under one or more of these leaders. The Chiricahua Apaches, among all the many North American indigenous nations, have been blessed with a surplus of first-rate leaders and warriors. When hard times challenged us, the right leader always stepped forward to help find a solution.

Chiefs have to be smart, savvy, tough, enterprising, skillful, strong, and indefatigable.

There were few hereditary chiefs. Each man who wanted to be a chief had to prove himself to the others that he was worthy of the position. It wasn't given to him. He had to earn it.

No warrior followed a leader simply because of his name, or who his father was. That warrior had to know, deep in his heart, that the man he followed was the best leader the people could possibly have under the circumstances.

Apache men served as warriors under the command of one of the chiefs. Geronimo was a medicine man and a warrior; he was never a chief. He led by example. He led because he was an astounding fighter. He led because he was wily and smart. He led because he was ruthless and cunning.

He knew how to lay a trap for the enemy that they couldn't possibly evade. He knew how to charge the enemy in such a way that the enemy couldn't draw a bead on him. He knew how to shoot and reload with such alacrity that he could lay down a solid wall of fire that forced the enemy to take cover.

He could make amazing things occur. The books and legends about him are packed with accounts of phenomenal events.

When the Apache were being chased by the Blue Coats and they needed a few more hours of darkness to make good their escape, Geronimo's medicine was so strong he could hold back the dawn.

He could make the Blue Coats think they were looking at a herd of cattle hustling along a trail instead of a ragtag band of Apache women, children, and old men racing for the protection of a deep arroyo.

I, Watson Mithlo, was a witness to these things.

Even in my mother's womb I was aware of what was happening.

I heard the screams, the shouts, the shots, the cries, the urgent snorts of the horses, the screech of the crows and the croak of the buzzards.

I watched the people as they boarded the train for the terrible ride to Florida and Alabama.

I worked alongside Geronimo and the other warriors at Fort Sill in the hay fields and with the cattle.

I was a member of the group that exhumed his body from the Fort Sill military cemetery and carried it in a sling with my compatriots and reburied it in a rocky crevice somewhere in the Wichita Mountains outside Lawton, Oklahoma. I, Watson Mithlo, was a witness to this.

I, Watson Mithlo, have lived, humbly and honestly, according to the codes and values of the Chiricahua Apache people.

CONGER

How to describe what took place that night? Nothing made any sense from a conventional perspective. It isn't enough to say that what transpired was bizarre or surreal or alien or strange; it's almost as if it's necessary to invent a new vocabulary to deal with the events that overwhelmed me that chilly night in October, on the dance grounds located outside the hamlet of Apache, Oklahoma. The roaring fire, the shadows of the dancers gyrating across the walls of the medicine tipis, the restrained whooping, pitched at a soprano-esque register, drowning out the drone of the musicians clustered around the bench.

I was testing, as best I could, my aversion to asking favors of anyone, particularly in regard to medical matters. It was early afternoon when I finally located Melvin as he was about to slip into his medicine tipi.

"There he is," Harry muttered. "Go speak with him."

I put on a brash face and approached Melvin; without thinking what it was I wanted to say, I blurted out at him, "Melvin, I need your help. My health is unraveling like a ball of yarn. Six years ago I was diagnosed with Parkinson's disease. Now I just learned that I have prostate cancer and will have to undergo radiation therapy. I'm a mess. Can you do anything for me?"

Melvin stared at me hard, the way that only Melvin can look at someone; the folds of his face bunched around his jowls. It was a stern face, serious and grim, the eyes stony and expressionless. I could only guess at what might be going through his head. He was a mystery to me. I couldn't begin to fathom the depths of who he was. I only knew that he had something I desperately needed.

It took a moment before he said, "You need to bring me the following items: a black kerchief, a knife with a blade that runs from the tip all the way through the handle, a Pendleton blanket, a supply of tobacco, and an eagle feather. You can give them to me once I'm inside the medicine tipi getting the boys ready to dance."

Harry came to the rescue. That afternoon we spent several hours running around Lawton, looking for the items. Melvin was nowhere in sight when we returned to the dance grounds around three o'clock. I busied myself helping Harry do some chores in anticipation of the visitors who would soon be swarming the dance circle. The folks in the cook shack were busy with their preparations.

"Now, before you hand anything over to Melvin you make four

gestures like you're actually handing them over, only you don't," Harry instructed. "You do that four times. After the fourth gesture you give them to him."

"When does that happen?"

"Just before the dancers come out of the medicine tipi."

The sun slipped behind a plump cloud poised on the western horizon like a stationary blimp. The October air had grown chilly; the temperature dropped as the wind picked up. Around the circle everything seemed casual and relaxed. People greeted friends and families; the greetings were warm and cordial, yet a bit restrained. The dance grounds were sacred grounds (or would be in a couple of hours). Harry sat in his chair next to the family's tent like a pasha, shaking hands with the people who came up to him. More than a cordial greeting he seemed unwilling to make.

He must work way ahead of himself, I decided. Or he must be incredibly well organized. Or he has a whole bunch of people at his beck and call.

"How do you manage to look so relaxed when I know you've worked so hard to put this on?" I asked.

"It takes a full year to mount an event like this," he replied. "Melvin and I know what to do, as do the ladies in the kitchen. The dancers have to train. They have to be in tip-top shape. Dancing for six hours takes it out of you. But once you've danced, you're not the same. You change. It's that deep and spiritual."

Here we were about to encounter the gods, and people were still going about the business of readying the dance grounds for the guests who would soon arrive in force. Apache spirituality must hover close to the surface, I decided, in access of those who need it most. The sacred and the profane cohabit this treeless site, working their magic within a very small space.

Melvin slipped into the tipi to busy himself with the dancers. I followed Harry for a while until he finally said, "You find Melvin and stick with him. He'll tell you what to do. You do everything he tells you to do."

The interior of the tipi was crowded with boys and young men dressing for the dance. Clutching my stack of gifts for Melvin, I backed through the opening and creaked around on my left heel. The air inside was warm and comfortable, laced with the scent of dried herbs and wood smoke and pent-up, adolescent energy. Melvin waved to me from his perch on the other side of the tipi fire and pointed to a seat next to him. I circled the fire in a clockwise fashion, located the seat, and sat down.

I went through the business of handing over the items to Melvin. Four times I offered him the sack. The fourth time he accepted it. Four is a sacred number for the Apache.

The climate inside the tipi interior was full of energy and anticipation. Everybody was working hard to get themselves ready for the dance. Punctuating this activity was the sound of the dancers conversing with one another in soft, throaty, dove-like murmurs. A modest pit fire popped and sputtered in the center of the floor. There was stuff scattered everywhere — headdresses, staves, buffalo robes, skulls festooned with feathers, quivers, arrows, swatches of animal fur. Melvin was painting sacred symbols and emblems on the backs and chests of the dancers. Just then Harry ducked into the tent and made his way slowly and deliberately around the congested space with the stately grace of an ocean liner. He greeted me with a solemn nod and handed me a hand-rolled cigarette. "Light it," he said.

A few pokes and I felt something inside me let go. Harry had disappeared. Inside the soaring tipi a different set of rules and imperatives held sway. This was another world that I was privileged to witness. And a witness was all I would be. We were about to partake of the buoyant, vigorous choreography of Indian dancing. With everyone ready to go, Melvin called for a song; the dancers responded with a host of squawky voices singing in a language few of them knew. One by one the dancers exited the premises until there was no one left but Melvin, myself, and two men. A third man slipped inside: Harry, checking on his protégé. I waved lamely at him, but he didn't respond. He came around the fire and sat down next to me.

"In a few minutes, Melvin will take you outside," Harry said. "He'll take you by the hand and lead you where he wants you to go. Trust him completely. He knows what he's doing."

I closed my eyes and took a deep breath. When I opened them, there was Melvin, staring at me, clutching my arm, his jowly face glazed with sweat. "Come with me," he said.

The night air was cool and invigorating. The stars appeared to have been wiped clean from the sky. But they were there, I could feel them; the light from the fire pits flaring around the circle blotted them out. The rim of the circle had filled up while I was in the medicine tent.

There were lots of people milling around, waiting.

"Let's go," Melvin said with a note of urgency.

He hooked his arm in mine and led me away from the tipi to a spot several yards behind it. "There's a chair for you to sit in."

A chair? I had no idea what to expect. The ground that Melvin steered me over was pebbly and uneven. I caught my toe and half-stumbled, but he held me steady; a moment later he settled me down in what looked like a striped lawn chair. "Sit still," Melvin whispered. "Don't say anything. The spirits are here. They want to welcome you."

I wasn't frightened—a little nervous, maybe. At the sight of me, the dancers commenced to jingle and shake and make an eerie, ululant sound deep inside their throats. On a stretch of level ground a few yards in front of me I saw something that caught my attention. The dancers were lined up in four rows at right angles to the chair in which I sat in the center of yet another circle. First the boys, then the teenagers, decked out in full regalia, their faces flattened by the sheath-like fabric of their regalia. A crash of music sounded behind me: men singing, praying, chanting, men tapping drumheads with willow sticks, men blowing shrilly on eagle-bone whistles. A confusion of sounds punctuated by a soft warbling as if from the throats of a covey of quail.

I watched dumbfounded as one dancer after another pranced toward me, high-stepping like deer, holding their staves above their shoulders, cooing and clucking. The closer they came, the higher they raised the staves with their wicked points, drawing them up to the height of the elaborate headdresses that pronged from their skulls. With a shout, the dancers flung the staves down, their points sticking in the ground a few inches from my shoes. Then, with an easy arcing movement, ducking and warbling, they whirled around and returned to the top of the circle.

The boys were different. They came up to me as gently as butterflies, fluttering about my cheeks and chin, grabbing hold of my hair and running their fingers through it. Four times they made this maneuver, each time coming at me from one of the four cardinal directions, the men clutching their staves, the boys loping like coyotes, reaching out to touch my face and wiggle their fingers through my hair. I sensed a build-up to something, what I did not know.

The last two dancers in the troupe administered the coup de grace. I don't know what else to call it. The first dancer approached cautiously, clutching something, which he quickly plopped down on top of my hatless skull. Reaching out with both hands, he worked the substance into my scalp, like a barber giving someone a shampoo. The next dancer then took my head by the ears and leaned over and with an audible crunch began to eat the substance sticking to my skull. My mind spun like a top. What in heaven's name was happening? Was this an effort on his part, symbolically at least, to heal me by eating the sickness! Back and forth the dancers swayed; the fourth and final time I nearly jumped out of my skin. They were so close, I could smell the smoke from the pit fire blazing in the center of the circle. The moment was excruciating. I wanted to cry out. Instead, I bit down on my tongue until the impulse passed; meanwhile, the dancers continued to wallow in the trough of my confused brain.

I could feel the presence of other people, gathered supportively around me, pinching my neck and shoulders in a gesture of solidarity. My flesh everywhere on my body was hackled with tiny bumps that twanged like taut wires. I shut my eyes, and when I opened them, the dancers were gone, flighty and evanescent as spirits are expected to be. Harry was nowhere in sight. A small crowd of people gathered around the chair, including Melvin; the music continued to shrill and pop, supercharged with energy and focus. A moment later, Melvin lifted my limp body out of the red chair and led me around the fire pit in an easy circle. "Now, Conger, here we go, one final circle around the fire, and we're done."

"I can't feel my feet," I grumbled.

"You don't need to feel your feet," Melvin shot back. "Don't look down. Your feet are just fine. Once more around the circle, and we're finished."

I pressed my arm against his. He squeezed my bicep with his free hand. A cool breeze lapped my sticky cheeks. The sky erupted in a cackling swash of stars.

Later that evening a woman I know, a white woman, came up to me as I sat under the pavilion next to Harry's tipi. "You don't know this," she said, "but one of the dancers looked as if he pried open your skull like the lid on a box, letting forth a splurge of tiny rockets that shot into the air and disappeared.

"I'm not kidding," she continued. "I've never seen anything like it, and I've been coming to these dances for years."

I saw Melvin one more time that evening; his mood was pugnacious and confrontational. "You tell them — the doctors, the lawyers, the politicians — all the rest of them other unbelievers — that you feel differently now. You know now there is something different between them and us and that difference has been and always will be a dividing line. Tell them that you know now we have been here forever, and we will continue to be. We are the First People, and now you are one of us. When they ask you who you are, you tell them that you are a Chiricahua Apache, alive and living right here. Right here. Now. In this place and time. You must be ever watchful; there are people out there who want to hurt you. They want you to do their bidding, and when you don't they have ways of fixing it for you. You tell them that you are here. That no matter what they do to you, they cannot take away the ground you stand on."

Melvin instructed, "I am here. Say it: I am here."

"I am here."

"I am here!"

"I AM HERE!!!" I roared.

He knocked my chest with the knuckles of his meaty right hand, making a loud clap like two plank boards being smacked together.

I was done. My body was limp. My mind swarmed with images of what I had just witnessed. Would I ever understand what it was all about? A burst of vigorous drumming clattered against my ears. The dancers continued to circle the field like prancing antelope.

Harry didn't talk much in the pickup truck on the way back to Lawton. I think he wanted a cigarette, which he could not have. He sat quietly, staring into the darkness, rubbing the fingers of his right hand across his lips.

Meanwhile, somewhere out in the Wichita Mountains, under a scree of shattered stone, Geronimo's body—a chunk of vellum curling at the edges like an autumn leaf—shivered and stirred. I turned my face away from the darkness and looked straight along the high beams of the pickup's bright lights for some kind of horizon line by which I could measure how far I had come, and how far I still had to go.

ABOUT THE AUTHORS

Harry Mithlo, enrolled citizen of the Comanche Nation and Chiricahua Apache son of Watson Mithlo, is an active cattle rancher. He is a retired educator who served on the Comanche Nation Business Committee as an elected official. He resides in Lawton, Oklahoma, with his wife Juanita Pahdopony in the heart of Comanche country.

Conger Beasley Jr. published over a dozen books, many dealing with the history of the American West. He won the Western Writers of America Spur Award in nonfiction in 1995 for *We Are a People of This World* and the Thorpe Menn Award for Literary Excellence in 1991 for Sundancers and River Demons.